# THE CASE FOR
# FAMILY WORSHIP

## *George Hamond*
### *(1620–1705)*

An answer to the question:
Upon what Scripture grounds and reasons
may family worship be established and enforced?

by
George Hamond, M.A.
Minister of the Gospel

Edited by Dr. Don Kistler

Soli Deo Gloria Publications
*. . . for instruction in righteousness . . .*

Soli Deo Gloria Publications
A division of Ligonier Ministries
P. O. Box 547500, Orlando, FL 32854
(407) 333-4244/FAX 333-4233
www.ligonier.org

*

*

ISBN 1-57358-169-0

*

Library of Congress Cataloging-in-Publication Data

Hamond, George, 1620-1705.
 The case for family worship : an answer to the question, Upon
what Scripture grounds and reasons may family worship be
established and enforced? / by George Hamond ; edited by Don
Kistler.
  p. cm.
 Rev. ed. of: A discourse on family-worship.
 Includes bibliographical references and index.
 ISBN 1-57358-169-0 (alk. paper)
 1. Family–Religious life. 2. Public worship. I. Kistler, Don. II.
Hamond, George, 1620-1705. Discourse on family-worship. III.
Title.
 BV200.H36 2005
 249–dc22

                                              2005006773

# Contents

iii

# Dedication

## To the Right Honorable Sir William Ashurst, Lord Mayor of the Renowned City of London

My Lord,

Should I have adventured to prefix to these papers the name of any other person who bears a character or makes a figure in the world, equal to that of your Lordship, it is likely that a large and well-contrived apology might scarcely have been sufficient to excuse my confidence. But so great is the civility and condescension of your Lordship that any honest man who comes upon a justifiable errand may find an easy access to you.

Your generous temper was a fair inducement, but that which was my principal encouragement to make this address to your Lordship was your long, serious, and unaffected profession of Scriptural and practical godliness. This was what gave me assurance that in presenting to you a discourse of family worship I shall only offer to you that which is familiar to you, and, by long and experimental trial found to be very consonant to the Holy Scriptures and the common principles of true piety.

If I should be so vain as to attempt to flatter a person of your worth and wisdom, I might not only be justly despised, but also derided because my Lord Chief Baron has publicly told the world much more of your character in a true representation of you than a sycophant could have counterfeited. And your actions at least confirm, if not exceed, all that which so great and

v

noble a person has spoken of you.

I had not, my Lord, any intention, by this dedication, to expatiate in the commendation of your virtues, nor any ambitious design to make myself thereby known to the world as presuming that whosoever should read your Lordship's name at the top would have the curiosity to see whose stood at the bottom. It is now too late for me to study such little artifices, for I have spent my life hitherto in no ungrateful retirement. And it would be to no small purpose for me to desire to show myself to the world (especially having nothing considerable to entertain men with) when, according to the ordinary course of God's providence, I am ready to leave it.

But the real reason why I was desirous that your Lordship's name should appear before this discourse, was the hope which I conceived that thereby some might be induced more seriously to consider the subject therein treated, which all must grant to be of great importance.

My endeavor to assert and establish family worship is an undertaking which, I am confident, all good men will allow of, and your Lordship will patronize. As for the failures and weaknesses which are too visible in the management of it, I promise myself that either your Lordship's candor will overlook them or your goodness pardon them.

Let others be as severe as they please in censuring, and as supercilious as they will in despising the composer, yet I shall be heartily thankful to those who will bring stronger arguments to prove, or more effectual persuasives to recommend, this excellent part of religion to all who bear the name of Christ in the world. I am almost assured that there are none who will directly and openly appear against it. And if men will use no other weapons than those of Scripture and right reason, I am perfectly sure that they cannot shake it. May God be better served by us in all capacities and relations, in our congregations, families and closets; and then the only design of these papers is attained.

May Almighty God afford your Lordship His gracious assistance and carry you through your eminent magistracy with prudence, integrity, and honor; and command His grace and blessing to rest upon your virtuous lady and all the branches of your worthy family.

And thus, my Lord, with your permission, I shall adventure to subscribe myself as your Lordship's very real, and not only your nominal servant,

*George Hamond*

# Preface

To all the religious worshippers of God in their
families, inhabiting in and about London;
particularly, to those of that congregation
in which the providence of God has set
me to labor in the Word and doctrine

It may be expected that I render some account of
myself, and of the reason why I direct this discourse to
you, because it is likely that I am known to compara-
tively few of that great number which I hope are comprehended in this inscription. I have, from my youth to
my gray hairs, been employed according to the grace
vouchsafed to me in ministering the gospel of our Lord
Jesus Christ, though in much weakness and manifold
failings, for which I humbly implore pardoning mercy
and hope for acceptance through the blood of Christ.
During those years in which I have exercised my ministry in this city, I have appeared but little out of the
limits of that congregation to which my attendance was
especially required, unless it were occasionally at the
morning exercises, and rarely to assist some of my
brethren. Neither have I been forward to print any
thing, being conscious to myself of my own insuffi-
ciencies; only I was under a kind of necessity to allow
two plain sermons to go abroad, one in the fourth vol-
ume of the casuistic morning exercises\*, the other a

---

\* The author is referring to those sermons which were published
under the title *The Morning Exercises*, or *The Cripplegate Sermons*.
These were last reprinted by Richard Owen Roberts of Wheaton,
IL.

funeral sermon for my respected and beloved brother
Mr. [Richard] Steele.

Now I am to send forth this discourse on family
worship. And I think myself obliged to let you know by
what steps I was led to the publication of it. Some
months since, another Reverend Brother [Matthew
Barker] and myself were desired by the United
Ministers to draw up a short account of the Scripture
grounds and reasons for family worship. This was done
by that other very judicious person. And I also offered
them some hasty, undigested thoughts about it. But afterwards I bestowed more time upon that subject, which
produced this discourse that I now present unto you,
not as coming from the United Ministers, but in my
own name only. And I desire that this may be well-
observed, so that it may appear that my brethren are not
responsible for anything that is faulty or defective
herein. If therefore any persons shall take exceptions at
what is here asserted, I hope they will be so just as to
level their displeasure at myself only. This is enough,
and perhaps too much, touching myself.

As for the reasons why I direct these papers to you, I
think my calling licenses me to declare (as I am able)
the whole counsel of God. Neither does anything that I
know of forbid me from assisting the children of God
for the furtherance of their knowledge, faith, holiness,
and comfort. Besides, I humbly conceive that this discourse may be proper for you and acceptable to you because it brings you no new doctrines, but the common
faith and practice of the saints throughout all the ages
of the church. Here you will not find anything to perplex your minds, disorder your affections, or waste your
precious time, in reading the fiery and endless wran-
gles of them who contend for glory or victory without
any great advantage to the clearing or establishing of
the truth. But in this small piece there is nothing to

disturb your repose or retard your progress in holiness. But, by the blessing of God, you may meet with something which may inform your judgments and engage you with greater vigor and alacrity to exercise yourselves in this excellent part of practical religion. This I think sufficient not only to excuse, but also to justify my making this address to you.

I have mentioned these things because I thought it decent to testify that respect which I have for you, accounting it would have been a piece of rudeness to have obtruded these papers upon you without some previous application—and also to ease any inquiries of some who may be willing to peruse this discourse, and, in order thereto, have a mind to know something touching him who drew it up.

But I confess the principal design of this preface was of a very different tendency than to apologize for this inscription, as an invitation to your reading of the discourse itself. For I resolved, upon this advantage, to lay a few things before you which I apprehend deserve your serious consideration. I hope that you will find something in this discourse that may inform and confirm your judgments that family worship has a divine warrant. Let me beseech you to persevere in the performance thereof with full assurance of faith. And if you meet with any suggestions that may unsettle you—whether they arise from your own darkness or weakness, or from the cavils or scoffs of others—you may fortify yourselves against their insinuations. Also, I entreat you to observe and fix in your minds such arguments for family worship as appear to you most plain and forcible, and to make use of them (as a fair occasion may be offered) to satisfy those who question or blame your practice. In this way they may see that you are not led thereto by singularity or affectation, nor merely from custom or the authority of your teachers,

but from Scripture grounds and directions, and the
common sentiments of all the children of God, and
their example in all the successive ages of the church.
Who knows but that your charitable and prudent management of such advantages as providence may put into
your hands may be blessed of God, so that the ignorant
or prejudiced may receive information and satisfaction,
and the mouths of the refractory may be stopped.

As I have endeavored to lay the solid and deep
groundwork upon which family worship is built and established, so I beseech you not to build upon it wood,
hay, or stubble (I mean a slight and superficial performance thereof), but that you would, as often as you are
employed in this holy work, be sure to preserve and excite that divine principle of grace which is planted in
you by the Holy Ghost, remembering (what is often in-
sinuated in the discourse itself) that family worship,
rightly performed, is truly and really divine worship.
And therefore it is to be always carried on with a pro-
found reverence toward the Divine Majesty, and with
great humility and sincerity as that which is to be offered up to the most holy and blessed God through
Jesus Christ the Mediator, by the aid and assistance of
the Holy Spirit. Bear with me, if in this matter I endeavor to stir up your pure minds with the uttermost ef-
forts of zeal and charity that I am able to put forth. For I
fear (God grant it may be without cause) that this part
of practical religion, as well as others, has suffered a
lamentable declension from its pristine vigor among
professors of religion. There are (God knows) too many
symptoms that the power of godliness lies languishing
and withering among us. Let us remember from
whence we are fallen, and repent and do our first
works. When men satisfy themselves with retaining the
images and pictures of divine ordinances, or holy exercises, and have either relinquished or lost the spirit

and vital power of them, the effects will be found to be very mischievous and dreadful.

Let me have leave to press you with a justifiable importunity to keep on; be constant and uninterrupted in the performance of family worship, and do not suffer it upon any pretension to be interrupted or hastily done. I confess, there may be some circumstances which may unavoidably necessitate the contracting thereof (for that time) in several parts thereof, so that the reading, prayer, etc., may be the shorter. But take heed that what may be allowed upon some rare and unusual emergencies and occasions does not betray you into a customary indifference of spirit, and so from an evil principle or habit your family worship becomes slight and short just so that you may gratify the world, or some inordinate affection and irregular passion. When you find these indispositions or prevarications gaining ground upon you, then, in the strength of Christ, excite and engage your hearts to greater sincerity and fervor in your family duties. Hold close to them, and do not allow them to start aside, like deceitful bows.

Here I must be allowed to give vent to that just sorrow and indignation which are stirred in me by observing how the spiritual distemper increases and eats into the vitals of religion. At first some continue the exercise of family worship in the external part, but with great remissness or indifference of spirit. Then, upon some real or imaginary necessity, they give themselves a dispensation to omit it altogether for once, and are not humbled for it if it were indeed their sin, nor are sensible of the prejudice which they sustain thereby, and so smart under it, as their affliction. At last, necessities and obstructions come to be so multiplied that family worship cannot find a convenient season to be entertained in for possibly two or three days. When it comes to this, the persons (to say the least) are certainly under a spiritual fever that lasts three or four days; for this cannot proceed from the spirit of a sound mind which is even and steady. That I may therefore contribute my best assistance to those who labor under this infirmity (supposing them to have the root of matter in them) and, by way of prevention, to antidote such as may be in danger of falling into it, I shall endeavor to impress upon your consciences the necessity of the daily performance of family worship.

When you thoroughly search into the Scripture grounds and reasons for family worship, you will find them to be as strong and prevalent to establish daily worship as the worship itself. For you may observe that our blessed Savior, giving directions about prayer, prescribed this petition: "Give us this day our daily bread." Here it is evident that daily bread must be daily asked for. It is not then sufficient that we pray for bread once a month, once a week, or every three or two days, but this must be done every day. And I doubt not but every serious person believes daily grace to be as valuable and necessary as daily bread, and that our souls want supplies as well as our bodies. I am willing to hope that family worship (of which prayer is an essential part) will be sufficiently asserted in the discourse to follow, and, if so by our Savior's determination, there must be daily family prayer.

Though the petition for daily bread includes all other things necessary for our supply and support while we are passing through this frail life, yet forasmuch as our blessed Savior is pleased to signify them under the name and notion of daily bread, and so to point to our daily repast, this may invite us to take notice of the ordinary stated seasons in which families usually come together to receive it. But in this we are not to be determined by national customs, which may be variable, nor by what particular persons may choose for their families, but by that which was the ordinary practice in those times and places of which the Scripture speaks. In it we find that their customary, stated meals were twice a day, and are called "dinner" and "supper." Luke 14:12: "When thou makest a dinner or a supper." The dinner time was in the former part of the day. Genesis 43:16: "These men shall dine with me at noon." The supper time was in the latter part of the day. Luke 14:17: "And he sent his servants at supper time." Hence it appears that the seasons of taking their common repast together were in the former and latter part of the day, which are in Scripture ordinarily called the morning and the evening, allowing to either of them a due latitude. This may be exemplified by one instance found in 1 Kings 17:6: "And the ravens brought him [Elijah] bread and flesh in the morning, and bread and flesh in the evening," that is, at the usual meal times of dinner and supper. That which I have to offer from what I have mentioned touching the ordinary meal times, which were twice in a day, is this: seeing we receive our ordinary repast twice a day from the hand of God's bounty, and our Savior teaches us to pray for our daily bread, may not this, without straining the words, be a fair intimation to us that family prayer should be performed twice a day? If any shall judge that this reason is defective in evidence or cogency, yet I am sure the invitation from hence to pray twice a day in our families is very allowable and pious, and on that account I may be permitted to recommend it to those whose piety may incline them to embrace it.

We have yet more clear and pregnant indications that God's solemn worship is to be performed twice in a day, and that the ordinary seasons for it are the morning and the evening. Only let it be remembered that the terms "morning" and "evening" are to be extended to their due latitude; for each of them contains the space of several hours. And yet they are to be so bounded and limited that they may be distinguished one from the other. This being premised, I shall produce some Scripture arguments to strengthen this assertion with great brevity, though the narrow limits of a preface will not allow me room to expatiate upon them.

We may collect so much from the disposal and determination which God Himself has made in His providence; for He has manifestly divided the day into the morning and evening, and has put a signal remark upon each of them. Psalm 65:8: "Thou makest the outgoings of the morning and evening to rejoice [or sing]," that is objectively, so that such as fear Him may be excited to adore and worship Him actively. Both these seasons for holy worship are mentioned conjunctly in Psalm 92:1–2: "It is a good thing to give thanks unto the Lord, and to sing praises to Thy name, O Lord most high. To show forth Thy lovingkindness in the morning, and Thy faithfulness every night." It is said distinctly regarding the morning in Psalm 5:3: "My voice shalt Thou hear in the morning, O Lord; in the morning will I lift up my prayer unto Thee, and will look up." And distinctly regarding the evening in Psalm 141:2: "Let my prayer be set forth as the incense, and the lifting up of my hands as the evening sacrifice."

The equity and reasonableness of morning and evening worship may be argued upon Scripture grounds. As for morning worship, common gratitude will engage us to praise God for his protection over us, and that rest which He vouchsafes to afford us in the night season. Lamentations 3:22–23: "It is of the Lord's mercies that we are not consumed, because His compassions fail not; they are new every morning. Great is Thy faithfulness." And both conscience and prudence will oblige us to pray for His direction, assistance, and

blessing upon what we undertake in the day. Psalm
104:23: "For then man goeth forth to his work, and to
his labor until the evening." And it is God's blessing
that causes us to prosper in our employments. We
should therefore pray, as Psalm 90:17, "Establish Thou
the works of our hands upon us, yea, the work of our
hands, establish Thou it." Regarding this, Abraham's
servant has set us a fair example to imitate in Genesis
24:12: "O Lord God . . . I pray Thee, send me good speed
this day." Thus did Nehemiah in Nehemiah 1:11:
"Prosper, I pray Thee, Thy servant this day." Commit-
ting our works thus unto the Lord is the most effectual
way to have our thoughts established (Proverbs 16:3).

As for evening worship, we are then to praise the
Lord, who has blessed our going out and our coming
in. We are to commit ourselves to His almighty protection. Psalm 4:8: "I will both lay me down in peace and
sleep; for Thou, Lord, only makest me to dwell in
safety." The inhabitants of this city (one would think)
should be very apprehensive hereof, who are so often
terrified by the breaking in of robbers, and the flaming
of houses on fire in the night.

Morning and evening worship may be enforced
from many Scripture injunctions which require us to
pray without ceasing (1 Thessalonians 5:17); that men
ought always to pray and not faint (Luke 18:1). "Let us
offer the sacrifice of praise to God continually"
(Hebrews 13:15). The meaning of such places cannot
be that we should do nothing else but pray, but that we
should not fail to worship God as often as He makes it
our duty so to do—and that will appear to be in the
morning and evening at least. For so we find the word
"continual," as it refers to divine worship, to be interpreted. Exodus 29:38–39: "Now, this is that which thou
shalt offer upon the altar, two lambs of the first year,
day by day *continually*. The one lamb shalt thou offer in

the morning, and the other lamb shalt thou offer at even." And then verse 42: "This shall be a *continual* burnt offering."

What I have here succinctly drawn up touching the daily worship of God in our families—that it be performed twice in a day, and that the morning and evening are the most proper seasons for it—I recommend to your serious thoughts, desiring you to keep these sayings and to ponder them in your hearts.

My fourth request to you is that you would exercise a holy prudence in ordering and determining the circumstances which are likely, in a special manner, to affect your family worship, both as to the place (if your houses afford you any variety for choice), and principally as to the time, which is always very much in your own power. Therein embrace all advantages that may promote it, and avoid whatsoever may obstruct or damnify it. Upon this occasion, I hope it will be excusable if I mention those complaints which I have heard from some who, in much anguish and grief of heart, have bewailed the disorderliness of many in the management of their family worship in the unseasonable timing of their evening duties. I hear that masters of families ordinarily stay out until it is exceedingly late at night, and that in the meantime some of their servants take the liberty to be where they should not, and in such company as instill into them the poison of levity, unfaithfulness, or debauchery; which having once taken root in them will not soon or easily be eradicated. I hear also that those who remain at home, expecting their masters to come in and perform the evening worship, are quite worn out, either by their labors in the day or the weariness of waiting, or the insuperable prevalence of natural infirmity, become drowsy, and are so indisposed that not only their minds and affections are dull and lifeless, but even their

senses are locked up in sleep (through the greatest part
of the worship) which, because they could not take sea-
sonably in their beds, they adventure to admit while
they are upon their knees. I do not bring this as an ac-
cusation or a reproach to any, but as a caution to all so
that the culpable may be induced to repent and reform
this disorder, and that others may be advised to be vigilant so that they are not entangled in the snare.

I most earnestly entreat you to take care that your
family religion be always seconded and cherished by a
holy conversation so that, as you set up the worship of
God in your houses, you would preserve the fear of God
in your hearts and manifest it in your lives. You distinguish yourselves from the carnal and profane by wor-
shiping God in your families; take heed that you become not the same with them in any of their evil practices. Religion will be sorely wounded and insolently
reproached if you give occasion to them who seek occasion to disgrace both it and you. I must also exhort and
beseech you to walk wisely in your houses, with perfect
hearts, so that your servants are not scandalized. It will
be a dangerous stumbling-block in their way if they
hear you speak with tongues of angels when you are on
your knees, and out of the time of worship hear you
speak as children of Belial, venting your distemper in
words of bitterness and railing, or observe in you the
unsavory belchings of pride or passion. Your evil example will then prejudice them more than your instructions and prayers will edify them.

I have one request more, which I hope I shall obtain
as soon as I propose it: that you would, in your family
devotions, strive earnestly with God that He would be
gracious to the church and state. Pray that religion and
righteousness may take deep root, spread, and flourish
among us; that under the reign of their majesties, the
righteous may flourish and an abundance of peace as

long as the moon endures. And do not forget the
churches of God abroad; plead the cause of despised
Zion against her insulting and potent adversaries; that
when the Lord shall have washed away the filth of the
daughters of Zion, and have purged the blood from the
midst thereof by the spirit of judgment and the spirit of
burning, He would create upon every dwelling place of
Mount Zion, and upon her assembles, a cloud and a
smoke by day and the shining of a flaming fire by
night, so that upon all the glory there may be a defense.

These are the requests which I earnestly make to
you, and the advices which I have taken the confidence
to lay before you, assuring myself that they will meet
with a kind reception from you. And so I commend you
to God, and to the Word of His grace, which is able to
build you up and to give you an inheritance among all
them who are sanctified. Amen.

# 1

## *The Introduction*

Before the case of family worship can well be clearly and satisfactorily stated, I humbly conceive that some general considerations touching the worship of God are to be premised, which I shall lay down as postulata, or propositions to be consented unto and agreed upon in this debate.

1. The eternal, living, and true God is to be worshipped by all. Psalm 22:27–28: "All the kindreds of the nations shall worship before Thee. For the kingdom is the Lord's, and He is Governor among the nations." Psalm 66:4: "All the earth shall worship Thee." Scripture testimonies may be spared because this is a principle engrafted in the natural consciences of all men, and professed by Jews, Mohammedans, and Christians of all denominations, yea, by pagans themselves, They, then, who deny or cast off the worship of God are worse than infidels and are to be ranked among the atheists. Psalm 14:1: "The fool hath said in his heart, there is no God." He who pays no religious worship to the Deity owns no God, and he who says that he acknowledges a God, but that he owes no worship to Him, entangles himself in a wicked and foolish contradiction.

2. Family worship, rightly and religiously performed, is truly the worship of God; for it partakes of the general nature of divine worship, is the same with it for substance, and has all the essentials of it. That it

comes to be performed in families is only accidental and a mere circumstance. They, therefore, who will not admit of family worship ought, in reason, to show either that it is not divine worship or that it cannot be performed in families, that the Scriptures may not be read in families, nor God invoked or praised, nor the members of the family be instructed in the knowledge of God, nor be exhorted to live soberly, righteously, and godly. These are the instances in which family worship is to be employed and exercised.

3. In order to the regular and acceptable performance of religious worship, it is necessary that the worshippers have in them the principle of grace, and that the same principle be duly excited, acted, and exercised. The principle of grace is required. Hebrews 12:28: "Let us have grace, whereby we may serve God acceptably." John 4:24: "God is a Spirit, and they that worship Him must worship Him in spirit and in truth." There are many other places. This principle of grace ought to be actually excited and exercised in all religious worship. Romans 8:26: "Likewise also the Spirit helpeth our infirmities, for we know not what we should pray for as we ought." Suppose there should be grace in the principle; yet if it is not stirred up, God does not account Himself to be acceptably worshipped. Isaiah 64:7: "There is none that calleth upon Thy name, that stirreth up himself to take hold of Thee." That prayer which is acceptable and successful must have the principle or spring of activity which is within, wound up, and set amoving. Hence it will follow that whensoever, wheresoever, or by whomsoever God is worshipped aright, the worshippers themselves ought to be godly, and to worship Him after a godly sort, with faith, sincerity, activity, and alacrity, and in the exercise of other graces. Psalm 103:1: "Bless the Lord, O my soul, and all that is within me bless His holy name." Psalm 145:18:

"The Lord is nigh to all them that call upon Him, to all that call upon Him in truth." All this belongs to family worship as much as to any other; though it may be feared that too many do not charge their consciences with it so closely and frequently as they ought to do.

4. Persons in an unregenerate or unsanctified state are not (while they so continue) in a fit capacity to worship God acceptably; and yet they are under an indispensable obligation (in point of duty) so to do, and are inclined to divine vengeance if they do not worship Him. The reason is evident: because man, being God's creature, must of necessity always continue under His realm and dominion. And being a rational creature, capacitated to know and serve Him, he is thereupon bound to worship Him. This will be clearly made out if we compare Acts 17:28 ("In Him we live, move, and have our being") with Psalm 95:6 ("Let us worship, and bow down, let us kneel before the Lord our Maker"). So that neither man's impotence nor impiety can divest God of His authority to require and command him to render Him that worship which is due to Him, and to punish him for his neglect and disobedience. This is evident from Luke 19:14: "His citizens hated him, saying, 'We will not have this man to reign over us.' " Here they renounce their allegiance; and though subjects de jure, or of right, yet they declare themselves to be enemies. Yet their rebellion could not secure them from the arm of justice, for it follows in verse 27: "But those Mine enemies, which would not that I should reign over them, bring hither, and slay them before Me."

From this hypothesis, two useful corrolaries may be deduced:

COROLLARY 1. The present state of every ungodly person is most wretched and deplorable. And it will appear to be so though we look no further than that intricate and perplexed condition in which he is involved and entangled, with respect to his worshipping God.

If he supposes that those performances which he tenders to God (under the notion or pretence of worship) will find acceptance with Him, he grossly deceives himself. For God has plainly declared that He despises and will reject the services of such as are impenitent and ungodly sinners. Proverbs 15:8: "The sacrifice of the wicked is an abomination to the Lord." Isaiah 1:13: "Bring no more vain oblations." Psalm 66:18: "If I regard iniquity in my heart, the Lord will not hear me." John 9:31: "Now we know that God heareth not sinners." Let the profane and hypocrites lay this to heart, and flatter themselves no longer with their own delusions.

If any, upon hearing that God abominates the worship of the profane and hypocritical, shall hereupon desperately conclude that then it is best or most eligible for them not to worship Him at all, they must know that casting off and renouncing all religion will not secure them from the vindictive justice of God, but is the way to pluck down more wrath upon themselves. Because by such contempt and contumacy they (at least by implication) renounce His sovereignty, yea, His very being, and bring upon themselves swift destruction. Psalm 73:27: "They that are far from Thee shall perish." Psalm 10:4: "The wicked, through the pride of his countenance, will not seek after God. God is not in all his thoughts." Jeremiah 10:25: "Pour out Thy fury upon the heathen that know Thee not; and upon the families that call not upon Thy name." Men may be guilty of many sins for which God will punish them, but when He gives an instance in one sin, we may conclude that one to be the most provoking, as in Amos 2:4, "For three transgressions of Judah, and for four, I will not turn away the punishment thereof; because they have despised the Law of the Lord; and their lies [i.e., their idols] have caused them to err." It is as if it had been said, "Their idolatry was the principal, meritorious, provoking cause of their ruin." Thus, when God shall arraign many for their blasphemies, excesses, uncleanness, and the like, this may be written in the head of their indictment: "These shall die because they have not called upon My name."

COROLLARY 2. Matters standing as they have been declared, with respect to the worship of God and the qualifications of the worshippers, we may infer that it is the duty and should be the care of all faithful ministers to charge all persons with whom they have to do to worship the eternal and living God; and also so to worship Him that they sanctify His name, and may find acceptance with Him through the Lord Jesus Christ. In dealing with them about this affair, they should accommodate their instructions and exhortations to the spiritual state and condition of their people. They should encourage, assist, and direct the godly to worship the Lord in the sacred assembles, in their families, and in secret, and to prove to the grossly ignorant, the profane, the worldly, and the sensual that they lie under an indispensable obligation (in point of duty) to worship the great God, their Maker, Preserver, Owner, Lord, Ruler, and Benefactor. They should denounce His wrath against all those who (under any pretense whatsoever) refuse or neglect to worship Him, and should seek to convince the impenitent and ungodly that (while they continue as such) they do but mock, affront, and provoke Him by their counterfeit and hypocritical worship. And thereupon they should press them (with all the fervors of zeal and tenderness, of compassion and charity) to repent and be converted so that their sins may be blotted out; to turn themselves from all their transgressions diligently to attend upon the ordinary means appointed and blessed by God for

the working of conversion and ingenerating of faith,
so that they may be reconciled to God by the blood of
His Son, and through Him to have access to the
Throne of Grace, and find acceptance both of their
persons and services. The ways of procedure herein I
must leave to the discretion, fidelity, prudence, zeal,
and compassion of those who desire to approve themselves good ministers of Jesus Christ, workmen who
need not be ashamed, rightly dividing the Word of
truth.

# 2

*The Question and the General Answer*

I shall now apply myself to the special consideration of family worship, and shall proceed by these steps. I take it for a fundamental, comprehensive principle that wheresoever the worship of God is rightly performed, it is always the same for substance, and includes whatsoever is essential to it. The worship of God may be distinguished and come under several denominations from some extrinsic circumstances. For we may speak of the worship of God as ministered in the sacred assembles, such as in Psalm 89:7: "God is to be feared in the assembly of His saints, and to be had in reverence of all them that are about Him." Psalm 111:1: "I will praise the Lord with my whole heart in the assembly of the upright and in the congregation."

We may also speak of family worship. Joshua 24:15: "But as for me and my house, we will serve the Lord." Acts 10:1–2: "Cornelius, a devout man and one that feared God with all his house."

There is also that worship which we may term personal, solitary, or secret. Matthew 6:6: "When thou prayest, enter into thy closet, and when thou hast shut the door, pray to thy Father who seeth in secret."

In all of these, the object, rule, and end of worship is the same. This should be minded by some who seem to be serious, composed, and devout in the public worship, but who are slight, superficial, and unconcerned in their family worship—as if public worship was the only substantial worship, and that which takes place in their families was only a ceremony or a complement.

To discourse of public or secret worship is not my present undertaking, and therefore I shall confine myself to Family Worship. I desire to discourse of it in its latitude or full compass, and so not to resolve cases or give directions about it, but only to endeavor to answer this question, as it was given to me: Upon what Scripture grounds or reasons may family worship be established and enforced?

The terms of the question, as thus framed, direct, determine, and limit the answer to Scripture grounds and reasons only, and therefore I shall not meddle with other precedents or authorities with which, if I had been furnished (whereas indeed I have not so much as sought after them), yet to have inserted them I conceive would be improper, if not impertinent. For to offer that which is not asked would be to obtrude a kindness which may be fairly rejected.

I do not apprehend that it is at all necessary or useful to spend time in the explication of the terms either of family or worship, because (as far as I know) the sense and meaning of them, as to this debate, is agreed upon, or at least is not controverted. And therefore, unless some new case may occur that will give occasion for a further inquiry into them, I shall presume that, as to the subject under present consideration, they are well enough understood. And so I shall enter upon my proper province.

QUESTION. Upon what Scripture grounds or reasons may family worship be established and enforced?

My answers shall be general, direct, and appropriate.

THE GENERAL ANSWER. It is evident from Scripture and (as far as I understand) acknowledged by all that, besides secret or solitary worship, there lies an obligation upon us (and that imposed by God Himself) that there ought to be social worship, which is to be performed by several persons conjunctly. Psalm 34:3: "O magnify the Lord with me, and let us exalt His name together." Acts 12:12: ". . . where many were gathered together praying." But I shall not call in more testimonies to confirm this position because I account it superfluous to be industrious in maintaining that which none (though otherwise of different persuasions) will (I think) dispute. The parties of all denominations admit of holy assemblies for public worship and grant that there are, and ought to be, particular churches, the respective members of which are to join together in the worship and ordinances of God, and that such churches are of divine institution. Here I might add that there are learned and godly persons who conceive that in the Scriptures there is mention made not only of congregational churches, but also of family churches. But I shall not at present form my argument for family worship from those family churches, but reserve our inquiry touching them for another place in this discourse. For I am now to debate the case with them who admit that church worship is necessary, but say they do not find any obligation or duty that binds them to family worship.

To these I offer this request, that they would assign some defensible reason that may satisfy others, as well as please themselves, why God should be worshipped in church assembles because they are holy societies of His own institution, very advantageously framed for the celebration of His worship and the mutual encouragement, assistance, and edification of the worshippers, and yet His worship be excluded from families, which are also societies, which owe their constitution to God, and are by their conjunction and the mutual relation of the members so disposed as to be exceedingly helpful to one another in order to the exalting of the glory of

God in their united worship?

In making this proposal I desire it may be observed that I am not now directly pleading the Scripture grounds and reasons upon which family worship may be established and enforced. And yet, if that which is now to be offered is thoroughly viewed and deliberately weighed, we shall (if I mistake not) find very much which may conduct to men's satisfaction about family worship. But I now suppose (and shall soon prove) that there is nothing so much as pretended to be drawn from the Scripture that has any shadow of disapproving or excluding the worship of God out of families. Now, is not this a very great settlement to a serious man's thoughts, and a confirmation to his judgment, when he understands that no opposition is made against his opinion or practice, either from Scripture or solid reason, even by those who declare that they do not concur with him in the one or in the other? A man would think a fortress to be in no great danger when those who come against it shall declare that they have no engines to batter it, nor ever hope to be masters of it, unless the defendants, either out of cowardice or treachery, will surrender it. A respondent would make no doubt of maintaining his thesis when the opponent shall tell him he has no solid argument to bring against it, but only a jest or a fallacy. What wise man would relinquish such a practice as he has by long and well-tried experience found to be exceedingly grateful, profitable, and comfortable, because another may say to him, "I cannot find fault with what you do, nor condemn it upon any Scriptural or rational grounds? I just do not find myself inclined or disposed to do as you do."

Thus far I have gone upon supposition. Now I proceed to prove that nothing can be alleged from Scripture or right reason against the regular and religious worshipping of God in families. What exceptions may be taken against the errors, indiscretions, or mismanagement thereof in particular instances or personal failings do not in the least affect that assertion which I here undertake or (at least) endeavor to maintain, as all unbiased and unprejudiced persons may easily perceive. And so I shall frame my argument from the nature and reason of the thing itself.

If the worship of God is not to be admitted into families, the reason must be either because that it is inconsistent with the nature of religious worship or because families are not capable of it or are unfit for it. But neither of these suggestions is sufficient to exclude the worship of God out of families. For it is no derogation to God's honor, nor debasement of His worship, that it is performed in families.

The glory and majesty of God is not thereby eclipsed or impaired. For though He dwells on high, yet He humbles Himself to behold the things that are in heaven and on earth. He has indeed myriads of holy angels who wait on His throne and worship Him day and night, and are incomparably better skilled in this excellent work than poor mortals who have their dwelling in houses of clay. Yet such is the wonderful and astonishing condescension of our most gracious God that He requires and accepts the worship of frail, sinful men, when rightly managed, of whatever rank or quality they are. The prayer of the poor, if it does not come from feigned lips, shall not be despised. For of a truth, God is no respecter of persons, but in every nation "he that feareth God and worketh righteousness is accepted of Him" (Acts 10:34–35).

And as this is applicable to persons, so it is also applicable to places. God will no more reject family worship because it is such than He will turn His face away from assembly worship. It is no debasement of God's worship that it is humbly and sincerely offered up to Him out of a poor cottage, if the worshippers mix it with faith, love, joy, and the exercise of other suitable graces, and then it is presented to Him sprinkled with the blood of Christ.

Families are neither incapable nor unfit for the worship of God if we look on either persons or places. The persons may be living members of the mystical body of Christ; they may have the aids and assistances of the Holy Spirit and be heirs of salvation. The places from whence it is offered cannot affect the worship, for our Savior has determined the case in John 4:21: "The hour cometh when ye shall neither in this mountain [that is, Mount Gerazim] nor in Jerusalem worship the Father." When God had chosen to place His name there, and that part of worship which was ceremonial or typical was mostly confined to the temple or Jerusalem, yet then might the moral or spiritual part of worship have been performed in their synagogues or in their houses. "I will that men pray everywhere," said the apostle in 1 Timothy 2:8. The prayer of Jonah, out of the belly of hell, mounted as high as heaven (Jonah 2:2). The midnight praises of Paul and Silas in the stocks (Acts 16) made a pleasing melody in the ears of the Lord. Very unaccountable then is the fancy and fond the superstition of some, who despise or neglect the worship of God in their families, and repair to the church to say their prayers (out of the time of worship), as if their houses were profane places and the church the only holy place that might sanctify their devotions.

Let us now sum up this evidence. Besides personal or solitary worship, the Lord requires social worship of several persons in conjunction. Families as well as churches derive their origin from God. There is not any Scripture or reason so much as even pretended to be brought against family worship. Neither is it inconsistent with the nature of religious worship, nor are families incapable of it or unfit for it. And, we may add, there are many commands that we should pray without ceasing and offer to God the sacrifice of praise continually; and God is to be worshipped in every place. Men ought, in all allowed ways, to do good as they have opportunity, and to govern their families in the fear of God. And then, upon the whole, we can put the question whether upon these and such-like premises we may not collect something considerable toward the establishment of family worship?

And yet we cannot fairly and quietly go on before we exchange a few words with some who stand in our way, who tell us that the foundation laid in the argument proposed is too weak and sandy to bear the structure of family worship if we should attempt to build it thereupon. Because, say they, though all that has been offered be admitted, yet the consequence will amount but to this only in the issue, that family worship is a matter of liberty, but does not prove it to be a matter of duty. Granting therefore that we may have family worship, yet it will not follow that we must worship God in and with our families.

To this exception I answer, this distinction between matter of liberty and matter of duty, as applicable to family worship, is by some owned and defended as their principle; and by many more adopted and taken into their practice, though they do not pretend to have any acquaintance with the principle itself. For it is manifest that there are those who will worship God in and with their families on the Lord's Day, and but rarely, if at all, on any other day throughout all the week besides. Others will allow God some worship once a day, and that, too often, very late at night, when many (if not most) of the family are under an utter indisposition for such holy work, but give themselves a dispensation to omit all morning service. What is the language of these practices but an echo to the cry of liberty and duty? It will be therefore necessary to examine this distinction before we let it pass; and, touching it, I have these things to offer to the serious and cautious.

It looks very odd and suspicious when it will intrude itself into those things wherein the sovereignty and glory of God, and the interest of men's precious and immortal souls, are directly concerned. Who is he who dares take upon himself to sort and range the commands of God, as it were, into several ranks and classes, and write on them, "These are matters of liberty and these are matters of duty," when He gives them forth with the same impress and stamp of His authority upon one as well as upon another? Deuteronomy 12:32: "Whatsoever things I command you, observe to do it; thou shalt not add thereto nor diminish from it." Matthew 28:20: "Teaching them to observe all things whatsoever I have commanded you." We are not our own, to determine of ourselves or actions, and say, "This we will impart to God, but that we will reserve to ourselves." But we must entirely devote and dedicate ourselves to Him, so that whether we eat or drink, or whatsoever we do, all must be done to the glory of God. It seems our blessed Savior was not acquainted with this distinction, but resolved all our obedience into a matter of duty. Luke 17:10: "So likewise ye, when ye have done all things that were commanded you, say, 'We are unprofitable servants; we have done that which was our duty to do.' " He who is at liberty to act or forbear, if he pleases to do anything for God in way of gratification, would be thought to oblige Him by doing more than out of duty he owed Him.

Let us inquire whether the distinction between liberty and duty deserves any better reception when it would insinuate itself among those things that con-

cern the welfare of our precious souls, either as to their
holiness or their happiness, such as when the power
and awe of the Word strikes our consciences, as speaking in the name and authority of God and says, "As He
who hath called you is holy, so be ye holy in all manner
of conversation. Having therefore these promises
(dearly beloved) let us cleanse ourselves from all filthiness of the flesh and spirit, perfecting holiness in the
fear of God. Abstain from all appearances of evil. Abhor
that which is evil, cleave to that which is good" (1 Peter
1:15; 2 Corinthians 7:1; 1 Thessalonians 5:22; Romans
12:9). Or when conscience is roused by those loud admonitions, "give diligence to make your calling and
election sure. Work out your own salvation with fear
and trembling. Seeing ye look for such things, be diligent, that ye may be found of Him in peace, without
spot, and blameless" (2 Peter 1:10; Philippians 2:12;
2 Peter 3:14). If such Scriptures as these penetrate a
man's heart and then this distinction whispers in his
ear, will all this tell you that here is a matter for your
liberty to be exercised about, but nothing of duty to
constrain you to it? Would not every serious Christian
who has any value for or care of his soul look upon it as
a temptation or imposture and reject it with indignation? Let this suffice for a more general inspection into
this distinction.

I shall now review it again, and impartially consider
how far it may be applicable to the case of family duties
now under debate. And here the nature of the thing itself will necessitate us to show the difference between
the circumstantials and the substantials of family worship.

With reference to the circumstances of it, a due liberty is not only to be admitted, but also to be asserted.
Of this I shall give two instances: the place and the
time. As to the place, family worship may be performed

in spacious houses, wherein there are several convenient rooms for it; it is perfectly indifferent whether it
is performed in the kitchen, the hall, or the parlor,
above or below stairs. In mentioning places, I am this
particular because there are those who have attempted
(at least shown their inclinations) to straiten this liberty and confine it to some appropriate place in the
house. Among others, Mr. John Gregory has a discourse touching the Upper Room, often mentioned in
the New Testament, from which he insinuates that in
every house (which can admit of it) there should be an
upper room sequestered from common uses, and ap-
propriated to religious worship, as the oratory or private chapel is in the houses of some great persons. But
this is to be wise (or rather to be nice) above that which
is written.

As to the time of family worship, it may doubtless be
performed at any convenient hour, either settled or var-
ied, and is not to be restricted to those hours which
some call canonical, to which some books for private
devotions have been adapted.

Touching both these circumstances of place and
time, I will insert my thoughts in four little aphorisms.

In both the places and times for family worship, certainly the most convenient are to be chosen, those that
are most agreeable to the solemnity of religious worship and most free from disturbances and distractions.

The governor of the family (if he is a person of an
honest heart and but of a tolerable, discreet head) is
the fittest judge and the most proper determiner of the
place and time when the family shall meet for religious
worship. Let him use but ordinary prudence, and I
think he needs not be at the trouble or charge to retain
a wise man who can resolve issues to resolve this one.

The faithful ministers of Christ ought to be very
cautious and tender in giving their advice, or laying

down rules about the ordering of the circumstances of family worship, and conform themselves to that excellent pattern which the apostle has laid before them in 1 Corinthians 7:35: "This I speak for your own profit, not that I may cast a snare upon you, but that which is comely, that ye may attend upon the Lord without distraction."

It is the piety as well as the prudence of private Christians, in all the circumstances of family worship (and in others of the like nature), to stand fast in the liberty wherewith Christ has made them free (Galatians 5:1). I add this caution: do not use your liberty as an occasion to the flesh, to patronize your omission or careless performance of your family worship. "Be not therefore deceived, God is not mocked."

I now proceed to the substance of family worship, and deny that the same liberty is to be admitted here that was allowed about the circumstances. For men are not at liberty whether they will worship God in their families or not, if it is apparent that it is their duty, which I shall endeavor to show in the sequel of this discourse. For the present, I think it enough that I tell such as think they may forgo family worship by making use of this distinction between liberty and duty as an amulet, that it is (in this case) but a broken reed upon which, if they lean too hard, it will certainly fail them and may possibly wound them. I hope then, that those with whom I am now dealing will not interpret it an act of unkindness, but as an instance of my charity, if I endeavor to wrest it out of their hands as far as it may do them harm. I confess that liberty and duty make a pretty sound in the cadence of the words, and that will go far with the injudicious, who are sometimes better pleased with the tickling of their fancies than the solid informing of their judgments. I know also that everything will be kindly entertained by some who are desirous upon any terms to be disengaged from their duty, which they suppose to be a yoke which too closely presses and pinches their necks. And yet, for all this, I am persuaded that some will not be so fond of this distinction when the insignificance and mischievous consequences of it (in this case) are clearly represented to them. I would therefore pray them to observe that which I now say.

Some who have begun with pleading their liberty (to the exclusion of their duty) with reference only to family worship have gradually advanced this distinction much further and extended it also to public worship in holy assemblies, and then to personal or secret worship, and declare that to use any of them is their liberty, but not their duty. And so it depends on their own good liking whether God shall have any worship from them, or none at all. And thus at last it will come to this issue, to quote Tertullian, " If God does not please a man, he cannot be God." This is a root of bitterness indeed, which has a natural aptitude to produce such poisonous fruit.

It seems somewhat strange and unaccountable, upon what inducements they are moved who bear the name and own themselves to be Protestants, to be so liberal in contributing to the maintenance of a distinction which is so nearly allied unto and so much befriends some wretched popish distinctions. Of such I shall produce two instances:

1. The Papists make their advantage upon that distinction which they have minted between Scripture precepts, which must be obeyed, and Scripture counsels, which a man may take or leave, observe or slight, as his inclination or interest shall determine. And if they can carry this, they will take care that Scripture precepts, which peremptorily exact obedience in point of duty, shall be as few as possible. This may be clearly

collected from a notable instance, for I think that it is acknowledged by them that it is a Scripture precept that we ought to love God; and yet several of them say it is sufficient that we do not hate Him. Others say that it is enough if a man puts forth an act of love, terminating on God as its proper object, once a year, or twice, or more; or once only during the whole time of his life. Though the Scripture is express, "Thou shalt love the Lord thy God with all thy heart, and with all thy soul," and so on (Matthew 22:37). If they can thus relax a Scripture precept, we may well suppose that they will take a greater latitude when they interpret Scripture counsels, which they say in their own nature leave men to a kind of indifference whether they will comply with them or not.

2. The Papists distinguish between works of duty and works of supererogation, which must furnish the pope's treasury with matter for indulgences.

If then the distinction between liberty and duty (as some make use of it) is such a dangerous tool, I think they should be persons of singular integrity and prudence who are fit to be entrusted with the custody and management thereof.

If any demand my reason why I spend so much time in sifting out this distinction between liberty and duty, I shall ingeniously and plainly answer that it was because in looking (as well as I can) through the whole subject of family worship, I cannot discover anything therein that can bear a dispute or debate with persons of understanding and sobriety but this, whether it is our duty to perform family worship, for all grant that we may. And nothing is or can be objected against it from the nature of the thing itself, as has been already manifested. So I leave that distinction to be employed by the forgers and framers thereof to what uses they please. In the meanwhile, I suppose we have gained one very considerable point by what is yielded us, that family worship may lawfully and warrantably be admitted into our houses. And if it is once let in, I hope it will maintain itself there well enough. And if it is conscientiously performed, I doubt not but that those who at first entertained it as a matter of liberty will judge themselves bound to continue it as a matter of duty.

This may suffice for a general answer to the question: Upon what Scripture grounds and reasons may family worship be established and enforced?

# 3

## The Direct Answer to the Question

I shall now proceed to the more special and direct answer to the question, having first premised that the grounds and reasons thereof are very many and of various kinds. And therefore it will not be sufficient, nor fair dealing, to single out any one of them by itself and say that it of itself is not clear enough, or is not cogent. But let them be taken altogether, and I suppose they will be of sufficient strength to make their way into the consciences of those who are susceptive of and will acquiesce in such arguments as the nature and reason of the thing itself will bear—no discreet person can in justice desire more. But what impression they may make upon such as, through ignorance, obstinacy, or sophistry, fashion themselves against Scripture and reason, I cannot know. Only I hope they will find nothing in them that may stir their temper or provoke in them the spirit of contradiction. And in this confidence I shall bring forth my arguments with all clearness and candor and dispose of them in the best order and method that I am able to manage them.

My first argument is taken from the most ancient and general practice of mankind. Here I suppose that maxim will be admitted that ancient precedents, with general customs and usages (in things good and in themselves lawful, useful, and profitable), are in some sort equivalent to laws, and that family worship in truth may be attested by the examples of both the bad and the good.

*Of the bad.* It is evident that both heathens and Jewish idolaters have maintained and used family worship. The heathen had their family gods whom they called domestic gods and protective gods. In their writings we find frequent mention made of the *Genii, Penates,* and *Lares,* or household gods, for whom they had in their houses, *Lararia,* which were as private chapels or oratories in which they daily performed their divine service, as is particularly reported of the Emperor Alexander Severus. That this was the ordinary practice of the heathen is not (that I know of) questioned by any. And as for others, both Jewish and Eastern idolaters, the Scripture intimates as much by making frequent mention of their *Teraphim.* For example, where it reports that Rachel had stolen her father's images, the word in Hebrew is *Teraphim,* which the Septuagint and vulgar Latin translate as "idols." These are generally supposed to have been, in both their nature and use, near of kin to the heathen's *Penates.* Micah had a house full of such gods (Judges 17), which were at first intended for family worship, though afterwards employed in a more public way in the tribe of Dan (see Judges 18).

OBJECTION. This which you call an argument for family worship deserves a worse name than that of frivolous and ridiculous trifling; to allege that precedents of heathen and other idolaters make a ground to erect Christian religious worship upon. Family worship is in a very tottering condition when it needs to be supported by such rotten posts!

ANSWER. The examples of pagans and idolaters may be alleged on various accounts and to contrary ends; for they may be propounded as patterns for imitation, or only produced as arguments for conviction. To propound them as patterns for imitation would indeed be scandalous, impious, and impudent, the Lord Him-

self having entered so plain a caution against symboliz-
ing with them in their idolatrous ways of worship in
Deuteronomy 12:30: "Take heed to thyself, that thou be
not snared by following them . . . thou shalt not inquire
after their gods, saying, 'How did these nations serve
their gods?' Even so will I do likewise." But to mention
them for the conviction and shame of those who are
called by God's name, and yet come short of heathens
and idolaters, is a strong, lawful, and convictive way of
arguing in which the blessed God Himself has gone
before us. Jeremiah 2:10–11: "Pass over to the isles of
Chittim, and see; and send to Kedar, and consider diligently, and see if there be such a thing. Hath a nation
changed their gods which yet are no gods? But My people have changed their glory for that which doth not
profit."

In like manner I propound my argument in the case
under consideration. Shall pagans and idolaters maintain a worship in their families for them who are no
gods, and shall such as own the living and true God exclude His worship out of their houses? This may administer a just occasion to cry out with indignation in
the following words from verse 12: "Be astonished, O
heavens, at this, and be horribly afraid." And so I leave
this argument to be further weighed by such as think it
may be blown away with a breath or a scoff.

*Of the good.* The second rank or order of examples
shall be of those against whose persons or practices (in
this case) no just exception can be taken. For they are
such as are celebrated in the Holy Scriptures for their
piety. This, as well as other things, is produced as an
example. They took care of the religious government of
their families, wherein they set us something to copy;
for in this case we may warrantably allege Romans 15:4:
"Whatsoever things were written aforetime were written
for our learning." In this argument the streams run fair

and clear from the spring of families in the world.

And now we are entering into a spacious and fruitful field, wherein we may meet with many rare examples of those whom the spirit of God has signaled out for their singular piety, fidelity, and industry in promoting family religion, some of which we shall more particularly contemplate as we pass through the gates of time under both the Old and New Testament.

In the Old Testament, in every remarkable period, we find the plain footsteps of family religion. For a long time after the world's creation, religion was formed in families only. The first mention that is made of any assemblies held for religious worship (beyond the limits of families) was in the days of Enosh. For so do many learned and godly persons understand that passage which is recorded in Genesis 4:26: "Then began men to call on the name [or to be called by the name] of the Lord," that is, to worship God in public assemblies.

Some, to weaken the force of this argument, suggest that the reason why the worship of God was then confined to families was merely accidental, because of the present necessity, the world being then but very thinly populated. But when the numbers of men were sufficiently increased, the worship of God was carried into the public assemblies and left private families.

The supposition that it was only the paucity of men that made it necessary that God should be worshipped in families is a very uncertain conjecture. For the creating of public assemblies for divine worship is admitted to have been in the days of Enosh. Then men began to call on the name of the Lord. This does not specify in what period of his life—whether to his youth, manhood, or old age—this is to be fixed; so that here is a great latitude, for he lived nine hundred and five years. Who then can tell to what numbers men might have been multiplied during that space of time? But if any will take the words in the most contracted and rigorous sense that they can possibly admit, and make assemblies for religious worship contemporate with the very day of the birth of Enos, yet the world was then 235 years old. This is a space of time large enough for the increase of mankind, possibly, to some myriads.

Whenever it was, the erecting of public assemblies was no sufficient cause why the worship of God should be thereupon ejected out of families. For the same reason that will conclude that public worship must supercede and discharge family worship will also evacuate all personal worship.

Ecclesiastical societies for religious worship no more disannul family duties or privileges than political societies for civil advantages or benefits. And I doubt not but if family enclosures were broken down and they were laid common, the civil government would soon run into confusion and ruin. And the like would befall church assemblies, if family rule and order were removed. Thus may that stumbling block be taken out of the way, and we may hold on our intended course.

Noah stands in the front of the second remarkable epoch, of whom the Spirit of God gives this character in Genesis 6:9, that he was a just man, perfect in his generation, and that he walked with God. This includes a conscientious discharge of relative as well as of personal duties, among which the care of family religion must be allowed a principal place, and in this case especially, when all flesh had corrupted their way upon the earth and their wickedness rose to such a prodigious height of impiety that men cast off all reverence for God and bid open defiance to Him. So then God brought the flood upon the world of ungodly persons and swept them all away. But the most gracious God had provided an ark for the safety of Noah and his household, in which they were shut up for a whole year. It would be monstrous uncharitableness to doubt whether Noah and his household worshipped God all that while; and yet it would be too much easiness and credulity (without better proof) to swallow down that fabulous tradition that at the break of every day Noah stood up towards the body of Adam (which, they say, he had with him in the ark) and before the Lord, he and his sons. And Noah prayed, and the women answered from another part of the ark, "Amen, Lord." To set forth this pageant with the greater pomp, they show us that very form of prayer which Noah then used. But we do not need these rabbinical fictions to bear witness to Noah's family religion; for it is evident that during the time of his stay in the ark, and for many years afterward, in Noah's family was the only audience in the world in which God was solemnly worshipped.

Abraham may well begin the third period. But before I insist upon his example to confirm what I intend to deduce from it, I think it deserves a special remark that the history of all the former Patriarchs is dispatched with unusual brevity, hardly to be paralleled in any who undertake to write the lives of renowned personages. But in writing the life of Abraham, Moses is very copious. And (which is most appropriate to our purpose) in delivering his memoirs to posterity, there is so much recorded touching his family religion that more clear and pregnant attestations thereto cannot reasonably be desired, neither need any more proofs to be sought after. Many things indeed are related of him which are both very admirable and instructive, and therefore may well excite us to fix our eyes upon him with the greatest intensity. He is called "friend of God," a title that dignified him above all the monarchs of the world. He is propounded as the great exemplar and father of all them who believe. Many are the rare in-

stances of his singular faith and obedience, but I shall
confine myself to his family religion, of which so much
is spoken as might afford plentiful and pertinent matter for a large discourse. But for brevity's sake, I shall
reduce what I have to offer to three headings: (1) God's
own testimony by way of approbation and commendation of him; (2) some instances of his family religion; and (3) the happy success and blessed fruits that
sprang from it.

1. God's own express testimony and singular commendation of Abraham for his family religion is
recorded in Genesis 18:19: "For I know him, that he will
command his children, and his household after him,
and they shall keep the way of the Lord." These words
being an oracle pronounced by the mouth of God
Himself, it becomes us to receive them with an humble
reverence, to ponder them with a stayed diligence, and
not suffer any of them to fall to the ground. Then we
may modestly, safely, and usefully draw forth these observations as naturally and freely issuing and flowing
from them.

The most high and glorious God, who always acts
according to the counsel of His own will, here conde-
scends to state this reason why He would not hide from
Abraham the thing which He was about to do. For He
says, "I know him, that he will command his children,
and his household after him." In other words, because
God knew that he would communicate to them what he
himself had learned from God; therefore he himself
should know more of His mind and counsel. Hence we
may infer that such governors of families as are most
faithful and diligent to instruct and to instill into those
under their charge those things which they themselves
have learned from God are in the most hopeful disposition to receive the communication of more light and
grace to their own education and comfort. Psalm 25:14:

"The secret of the Lord is with them that fear Him, and He will show them His covenant."

God said of Abraham, "I know him." The Lord is said in Scripture to know persons and things, either in a way of intuition (Isaiah 66:18: "I know their works and their thoughts"; Psalm 139:2: "Thou knowest my down-sitting and mine uprising; Thou understandest my thought afar off") or in a way of approbation, such as in Psalm 1:6: "The Lord knoweth the way of the righteous." In this sense, the Lord said that He knew Abraham as one who would afterward give sufficient evidence and demonstration of his integrity. In another instance, when Abraham, upon God's command, was ready to have offered up his son Isaac, Genesis 22:12 says, "Now I know that thou fearest God, seeing thou hast not withheld thy son, thine only son from Me." And here it is, "I know that Abraham doth truly fear Me because he will command his children and household to keep the way of the Lord." Hence we may learn that this is one way whereby we may approve ourselves to be such as truly fear God, if we conscientiously mind and promote family religion.

Here is the ratification of the godly man's charter, which invests him with power and authority to rule his own house, and to command those who are under his charge to keep the way of the Lord. *Praecipiet* is how the word is generally rendered. He will give them holy "precepts," rules and directions, and seriously and frequently inculcate them so that they may make deeper impression, as God Himself directs them to do. Deuteronomy 6:7: "And thou shalt diligently teach them unto thy children." The original word signifies "to whet," as it is rendered in the margin, a metaphor taken from sharpening iron tools, which was done by drawing the file backward and forward upon them. 1 Samuel 13:21: "Yet they had a file for the mattocks." The good ruler of his family must then be a diligent and constant teacher of his household. The Syriac version renders these words "he shall exhort them," which denotes vivacity, zeal, and affection. Our own translation interprets the word as "He will command," which directly imports authority and power. And in this case it is just and necessary (as was said upon another occasion, Esther 1:22) that every man should bear rule in his own house, and as a governor there, to encourage and reward the tractable and to restrain and correct the refractory if need requires. The failure and remissness of Eli herein was severely punished. 1 Samuel 3:13: "For I have told him that I will judge his house forever; for the iniquity which he knoweth; because his sons made themselves vile, and he restrained them not."

Abraham's care and fidelity was very exemplary; his command was to be laid both upon his children and upon his household, that is, all others in his family who did not come within the relationship of children. Discreet and religious parents must not, out of indigence or fondness, let loose the reins of children's extravagancies, but keep them strictly under family orders. And again, children, as being nearer and dearest to affectionate parents, must be their first care; accordingly, parents should use the greatest diligence to bring them up in the nurture and admonition of the Lord—therefore they are set in the first place. Note further that the household, that is, servants or others, must not be excluded or neglected, but kept under family rule and order, both they who stand in the upper and in lowest places in the family.

Here is at least an implicit promise of success and blessing on the faithful exercise of family government. "And they shall keep the way of the Lord," which is more fully expressed in Proverbs 22:6: "Train up a child in the way he should go; and when he is old he will not depart from it."

I shall close these observations with the apostle's enforcement and encouragement from 1 Corinthians 15:58: "Therefore, my beloved brethren, be ye steadfast, unmovable, always abounding in the work of the Lord, forasmuch as ye know that your labor is not in vain in the Lord."

Insisting so long upon this first part, God's own approbation and commendation of Abraham for his care of family religion, I hope may be justly excusable because it asserts the very life of the subject with which I am now dealing.

# 4

## *The Example of Abraham*

I will now produce some instances of Abraham's care about family religion, and how it was exercised and evidenced. Of these I shall mention three:

• Abraham's care was to bring all his household under the bond of God's covenant, and to fix upon them the seal of it. This he did by God's immediate and special command, as is related in Genesis 17 where is set down God's institution and then Abraham's ready obedience of faith in the observance of that institution. Verses 26–27: "In the selfsame day was Abraham circumcised, and Ishmael his son. And all the men of his house, born in his house, and bought with money of the stranger, were circumcised with him." The females were included in the males, and so all of them were brought into covenant with God. I do not doubt but that the exercise of family religion ought to stand upon this foundation, that they who worship God there together are supposed to be such as have taken the Lord for their God. Otherwise it is not to be expected that they who will not devote and dedicate themselves unto the Lord will ever conscientiously serve Him. This order the Apostle Paul declares in Acts 27:23: "The angel of God, whose I am, and whom I serve."

We may further observe that God Himself made provision in this matter, that none should celebrate the Passover (which was to be eaten in their several houses apart) until all their males were circumcised. Exodus 12:48: "And when the stranger shall sojourn with thee, and will keep the Passover of the Lord, let all his males be circumcised; and then let him come near and keep it." Otherwise, even the heads of the families themselves were not in a present capacity for it. Our blessed Savior imitates the like order in Matthew 28:19–20: "Go teach all nations" [or rather, make them disciples], as it may be explained from John 4:1, that Jesus made and baptized more disciples than John. This making of disciples was done by their solemn dedication to God by baptism; and then they were to be trained up in the school of Christ, and to be taught to observe all things that Christ commanded. This is a matter of very sad consideration, and should be well pondered by such as retain those in their houses (where all should join in the worship of the living and true God) who are not brought into the bond of the covenant. And yet their possessors neither endeavor nor desire to have them translated from the power of darkness to the Kingdom of Christ, but leave them without any regard or pity to perish in their unbelief.

Upon this occasion I hope I may mention without offense that it is commonly reported (how truly I do not know) that many of those who refuse baptism for their children are very defective or remiss in all the parts and duties of family worship. If this book should fall into the hands of any of that persuasion, I entreat them to esteem me not their accuser, but their monitor. And lastly, where all the members of the family are already dedicated to God by baptism, I must beseech them to be true to their baptismal vow and engagement, which binds them to be sincere and hearty in all the ways wherein they worship God, and not to satisfy themselves with the profession and form of godliness, but to act from an experimental feeling of the power of it.

This may suffice for the first instance of Abraham's care about family religion.

• The second instance is his frequent building of altars and offering sacrifices. Genesis 12:7–8: "And the Lord appeared unto Abram, and said, 'Unto thy seed will I give this land'; and there builded he an altar unto the Lord, who appeared unto him. And he removed thence unto a mountain on the east of Bethel, and there he builded an altar unto the Lord and called upon the name of the Lord." And then chapter 13:18: "Then Abram removed his tent, and came and dwelt in the plain of Mamre, which is Hebron; and built there an altar to the Lord." And so it is in other places.

Upon this instance I shall leave these remarks:

First, wherever Abraham resided with his family for any considerable time, there he used to build an altar.

Second, altars were always intended for the offering of sacrifices upon them; and that sacrificing was one of the most solemn rites by which God was then worshipped. 1 Samuel 1:3: "And this man [Elkanah] went out of his city yearly, to worship and to sacrifice unto the Lord."

Third, when sacrifice was offered, the whole family was interested therein and participated in the worship. This may be evidently collected from that which we find recorded touching Jacob's building an altar and offering sacrifice at Bethel in Genesis 35:1–3. The sum whereof is this: God, in giving forth His command, directs it to Jacob alone. Verse 1: "God said to Jacob, 'Arise, and go to Bethel, and dwell there and make there an altar unto God.' " Jacob understood the mind of God that this concerned his family as well as himself, and that he must have them with him. Verse 3: "Let us arise and go to Bethel." And accordingly he took effectual care for the reformation, preparation, and sanctification of his whole family. Verse 2: "Put away your strange gods; be clean, and wash your garments," that they might be in a suitable and fit capacity to join together in the sacrifice. His counsel had a happy success according to verse 4: "and they gave to Jacob all their strange gods."

I commend Jacob's practice as an excellent pattern to such as desire to maintain family worship in purity and power. Family reformation will greatly befriend family religion. And I shall enforce this with Zophar's advice to Job found in Job 11:13–15: "If thou prepare thine heart, and stretch out thine hands toward Him. If iniquity be in thine hand, put it far away and let not wickedness dwell in thy tabernacles. For then shalt thou lift up thy face without spot. . . ." The whole matter being thus set forth, I conceive it to be a pertinent instance of Abraham's care of family worship.

• The third instance is his praying for those of his family, which we may very probably collect from that which is expressly affirmed that he did in behalf of his son Ishmael. Genesis 17:18: "And Abraham said unto God, 'Oh, that Ishmael might live before Thee.' " It was a short petition, but comprehensive of all that a holy father can ask for his child. For to live before God is in effect that he may be graciously sanctified and eternally saved. Thus to walk before God is to serve Him in holiness and righteousness. Genesis 17:1: "Walk before Me, and be thou perfect!" To be eternally blessed is to be in God's presence. Psalm 16:11: "In Thy presence is fullness of joy; at Thy right hand are pleasures forevermore." 1 Thessalonians 4:17: "So we shall be ever with the Lord." Thus did Abraham pray for his son Ishmael, and we ought not to doubt but that he did as much for his only son (that is, by promise) Isaac, whom he loved. Nay, further, charity (which hopes and believes all things) will think of probable arguments such as his zeal, affection, and compassion sufficient to induce us to conclude that he did so for the rest of his family also.

Someone may object that if it were admitted that

something may from thence be deduced to favor that practice of a man's praying for his family, yet will it not reach that which they who urge the duty of family worship principally respect, and that is praying with our families.

To that objection I answer, that might have been observed to be established in the former instance, of the whole family's meeting and joining together at the sacrifice (as was there shown), and there Abraham prayed with his family, as is witnessed in Genesis 12:8: "He builded there an altar, and called upon the name of the Lord."

But if any seek for a particular example, haply we may find one, though not in the history of Abraham, yet in that of Isaac, the inheritor of God's promise and of his father's piety, who prayed not only for, but also with his wife Rebekah. This may more clearly appear if we make a due inspection into Genesis 25:21: "And Isaac entreated the Lord for his wife." Arius Montanus, keeping more exactly to the Hebrew, translates the words "over, against, or in the presence of his wife." He is not referring it to the person prayed for, or the subject matter of his prayer, but the disposing or the placing of himself when he prayed. Tremellius and Junius, indeed, render the words "his wife being present and together with him." What was collected from the family's joining together in the sacrifice, I judge a good proof for family prayer; and therefore I shall not insist upon this instance of Isaac, but having mentioned it I shall leave it to be further searched into by the learned.

3. The third thing to be observed from that which is recorded in the Scripture touching Abraham's example to encourage family religion was the happy success and excellent fruits which, by God's blessing, sprang from his religious and pious endeavors to promote it.

This appeared in general. All Abraham's servants wore the honorable badge of their master's piety, for they are called his trained servants, or, as it is in the margin, his instructed servants (Genesis 14:14). Arius Montanus translates "initiatos" as a word peculiarly applied to those who are instructed in and admitted to the sight or participation of religious mysteries. It is the same word that is used in Proverbs 22:6: "Train up a child in the way he should go, and when he is old he will not depart from it." The word is used to signify dedication in 2 Chronicles 7:5: "So the king and all the people dedicated the house of God." Thus were all Abraham's children and servants dedicated to God when they were entered into covenant with Him by circumcision. It is also used to signify instruction in the first principles, which is by the Greek called "to catechize"; so you may say, his catechized servants. This is one excellent use and exercise of family religion, to have all who need it to be well-instructed and grounded in the catechism. For my part, I conceive it far more probable that Abraham trained up his servants in the principles of religion than in military discipline.

More particularly, the success of Abraham's care for family religion most eminently appeared in the prudence and fidelity of his eldest servant, the steward of his house (who is supposed to have been Eliezer, mentioned in Genesis 15:2). With what admirable piety and dexterity did he manage that most important affair of fetching a wife for Isaac from Padam-Aram! The history of that we may read in Genesis 24.

Having thus passed through those three things touching Abraham's family religion, and laid the groundwork, I think that I may affirm with a modest confidence that we have a very good argument for family worship from Abraham's example, which will be yet more evident if we further observe that I have not alleged any one thing relating to his family's religion that carries in it any intimation that he acted therein by an extraordinary call or special dispensation, but that he went upon such grounds and principles as are common to all the children of God. For they have all the same Spirit to sanctify and lead them. Romans 8:14: "For as many as are led by the Spirit of God, they are the sons of God." They are partakers of the same saving graces as to the substance and kind, though not to the same degree. 2 Peter 1:1: ". . . to them that have obtained like precious faith with us." They walk by the same rule. Philippians 3:16: "Let us walk by the same rule; let us mind the same things." Galatians 6:16: "And as many as walk according to this rule, peace be on them." They are heirs of the same promises and shall partake of the common salvation.

The examples of the eminent saints, especially such as are recorded in Scripture for our imitation, lay more than an implicit and virtual obligation upon us. For we are expressly commanded to follow them in 1 Corinthians 11:1: "Be ye followers of me, as I also am of Christ." 2 Thessalonians 3:7: "For yourselves know how that ye ought to follow us." Hebrews 6:12: "That ye be not slothful, but followers of them who through faith and patience inherit the promises." James 5:10: "Take the prophets . . . for an example of suffering affliction, and of patience."

And so I shall close my argument for family worship as drawn from the example of Abraham, and leave it to the impartial and judicious to determine in the fear of God whether or not there is on Scripture grounds reason for the establishment and enforcement of it.

# 5

## *The Example of Job Begun*

The first period we examined was the time of creation, the second was that of Noah, the third of Abraham, and I shall now lay the fourth period, from Abraham until the time that the children of Israel were settled in the "land of promise." And in this interval I shall produce the example of Job, because many learned men refer his history to the time of Israel's sojourning in the land of Egypt. He was, doubtless, a most rare and excellent person, of whom the Holy Ghost gives so honorable a character not because of his plentiful estate, but because of his singular piety. Job 1:8: "And the Lord said unto Satan, 'Hast thou considered my servant Job, that there is none like him in the earth, a perfect and an upright man, one that feareth God and escheweth evil?' " He was a peerless person, whose equal was not to be found on earth. To him was that grace (in a good measure) vouchsafed which we are taught to pray for in that petition, "Thy will be done on earth as it is in heaven." After all this, is it not very remarkable and surprising that the first instance which is mentioned of his transcendent piety should be his religious care of his family? But so it was, as we see in verse 5: "And it was so that when the days of their feasting was gone about, that Job sent and sanctified them, and rose up early in the morning and offered burnt offerings, according to the number of them all. For Job said, 'It may be that my sons have sinned, and cursed God in their hearts.' This did Job continually."

Before I address myself to the improvement of Job's example as very appropriate to my present subject, I must endeavor to remove one stumbling stone or rock of offense. It is not unlikely that some, when they hear Job thus declare himself touching his sons ("it may be they have cursed God in their hearts") will be ready to suppose them to have been a crew of hell-bound, sensual epicurians, or desperate atheists, strange and unheard-of-monsters in a family of barbarians themselves, and must be looked upon as incarnate devils in a family that carries but the least shadow of being religious. But notwithstanding that expression here used (of cursing God in their hearts), I believe that Job suspected nothing worse of them than what might possibly by surprise, infirmity, or temptation befall persons in a regenerate state, though that which might be intended by those words is granted to signify something what is exceedingly sinful. Generally all interpreters tender those words in a more mild and mollified sense than the sound of them carries in it. It is most certain that the original said "and have blessed God in their hearts," but it is also evident that the proper sense of "blessing God" cannot be intended, for the scope and tenor of Job's speech will not allow for such a reading as this: "It may be my sons have sinned, and blessed God in their hearts." Therefore he undoubtedly intended by that phrase something that is evil whereby God might be provoked; and accordingly he has recourse to a sacrifice for expiation and to make atonement. Interpreters, both ancient and modern, use softer terms than that of cursing God. The Chaldee says, "It may be they have provoked God in their minds." The Syriac says, "They have offered some reproach to God," possibly by some irreverent or unsuitable conceptions of Him. Or, as Tremelius and Junius express it in their annotations, "They have not sancti-

fied Him as was fitting." But the prosecution of this any
further would be an unnecessary digression from the
design of this discourse. The Holy Ghost has not
branded them for any enormous crime; it would then
be an unjustifiable rashness to put a damnatory sen-
tence upon them. Bildad indeed casts in a malevolent
insinuation in Job 8:4: "If thy children have sinned
against him, and He hath cast them away in their
transgression." But little regard is to be had of the un-
charitable censure of him who presumed to condemn
Job himself, whom the holy and blessed God justified
and praised.

I shall therefore dismiss any further inquiry into
this matter, subjoining only these practical notes:

• Not only enormous and scandalous sins need a
sacrifice, that is, the blood of Christ, for their expiation, but also secret or heart sins. Acts 8:22: "Repent
therefore of this thy wickedness, and pray God, if perhaps the thought of thine heart may be forgiven thee."
And thereupon, enforce the apostle's exhortation
found in 2 Corinthians 7:1: "Let us cleanse ourselves
from all filthiness of the flesh and spirit, perfecting holiness in the fear of God."

• Job calls all forgetfulness, neglect, or contempt of
God, though but lurking in the heart and not openly,
or impudently declaring themselves to the view of the
world "a cursing of God." And hence we may learn that
godly persons so represent their own sins, and the sins
of those in whom they are most nearly concerned, as
exceedingly sinful and horrid, to excite their repentance and to beget in them an abhorrence for them.
Hypocrites, however, usually study extenuations and
diminutions for their sins to make them appear less
culpable, so that they may retain them more quietly
without disturbing their carnal peace and security.

• Such godly persons as desire to maintain family

religion in its power and vigor should be very tender and solicitous lest anything be found in their families whereby God may be dishonored, or provoked to suspend or remove His usual graces and favors from them.

So that nothing may be left to interrupt or perplex our intended argument for family worship to be taken from Job's example, there is one little objection more that may call for an answer:

OBJECTION. Job's sons are not to be reputed members of his family because they had their own houses, as is expressly said in verse 4: "And his sons went and feasted in their houses, every one his day." This will enfeeble, if not overthrow, the very foundation of any argument for family worship that shall be raised from Job's example.

ANSWER. When we seek to determine what it is that constitutes a family, we are not to seek for the causes thereof in the walls or enclosures wherein families may repose themselves. For then the nomads, who had no houses, could not have any families, which is a ridiculous supposition. If it were determined that where there are no fixed habitations there can be no families, we must dissolve and dissipate all the families of the holy patriarchs, at least as long as they were in such a moving condition as is described in Psalm 105:13, when they went from one nation to another, from one kingdom to another people.

The formal cause that constitutes and denominates a family is the relation in which the head and members stand toward each other. And accordingly, a family is described to be a particular or lesser society consisting of children and servants, under their proper head or governor, obliged to discharge the respective duties which they owe towards each other in their various places or stations. The head is the husband and wife. Concerning the husband, there is no question. And the apostle allows to the wife also a subordinate, governing power. 1 Timothy 5:14: "I will that younger women marry, guide [or govern] the house," that is, the family.

The mentioning of several houses belonging to Job's sons will not conclude them to be no members of his family, although they might have had wives and children; the Scripture does not assert this, but rather intimates the contrary. For all that is said touching the entertainments which were made all passed between the brothers and sisters. This may require a little more to be added to clearing what is essential to a family, which I think the more necessary, because it is likely we may be put upon it again in another place of this discourse.

Let it then be remarked that it is no unusual thing for princes and great personages to assign their children various apartments in their palaces or houses. And, as for their servants, who knows but that many of them may be fixed servants in one family and yet have houses, wives, and children of their own. And so, on different grounds, they may be both masters and servants as well as the same person may be a father and a son.

It need not seem strange that Job's sons had their own houses, such as they were, for I suppose that men's fancies must provide the materials, and be themselves the architects, who would build for them magnificent structures. These houses in all probability were but like those in use in those younger days of the world, some kinds of tents or of similar structure, which might be either touching each other or at some small distance from each other. I am more confirmed in this opinion by what we find touching the disposal of other families in those early days. Abraham had his tent, as we may collect from Genesis 23:2: "And Sarah died in Hebron, and Abraham came to mourn and weep for her." He came, I suppose, from his own tent. Express mention is made of Sarah's tent in Genesis 24:67: "And Isaac brought her [Rebekah] into his mother Sarah's tent." To "give full measure, and running over" to demonstrate that having distinct, appropriate places of repose was a very common thing for persons of one and the same family, let us cast cast our eye on Genesis 31:33: "And Laban went into Jacob's tent, and into Leah's tent, and into the two maid servants' tents, but found them not." This is referring to his images, or *Teraphim*, which Rachel had stolen. Then went he out of Leah's tent and entered Rachel's tent. I believe it will be no disreputation to Job's sons if we imagine that their houses were of some alliance with the tents—if not in their structure, yet in their use. And I am very confident that none will question whether Jacob's wives were of his family, although they had their own tents or houses, for it would be no unpardonable error to call them so.

Let not any fear that if we admit Job's son (who had their own houses) into Job's family, we should increase it to an overly great number. For it seems that in those days of sobriety and orderliness, such a family as Abraham's was, wherein were 318 who bore arms (and we may reasonably allow double the number to have been in his family) might be better provided for and more regularly governed (for they were his catechized servants who went out with him, as was before touched upon) than most families are among us, though they do not amount to the tenth part of that number. And further, it is obvious to every eye that in those days the stock had usually all the branches that grew out of it still cleaving to it. Jacob, with his twelve sons and all their wives, children, and servants, were but one house or family when he went down into Egypt. Genesis 46:26: "All the souls of the house of Jacob which came into

Egypt were threescore and six."

Having thus removed these two obstacles, I hope we shall not be troubled with any more, but that we may have our passage open and smooth. And yet, in our setting forth, I think it is but fair dealing that I acquaint the reader that I foresee our discourse upon the example of Job is likely to be of some length, and a pretty large compass. But I shall endeavor so to bound it that it shall not wander outside the just limits of my subject. I shall then entreat the serious and pious reader (if he thinks these papers may contribute anything toward his information or edification), that he would please go along with me patiently, and I shall undertake (as far as my poor capacity is able to judge) that in our progress we shall meet with many things which may contribute much toward the establishment of family religion; and also, several instances, according to which it is to be exemplified and exercised. And so under the guidance and assistance of the Word and grace of Christ, let us set out.

# 6

*The Example of Job Continued*

I esteem it a good omen that the first thing which presents itself to our view is so exceedingly amiable. From Job 1:4 we see that Job's children lived together in sweet accord and entire amity, and that they entertained one another with reciprocal kindness. This is a blessing which all families are not so happy as to enjoy. But doubtless it is a mercy in itself for its excellent fruits; and consequently it is very desirable and delightful. The psalmist was ravished by the contemplation of it. Psalm 133:1: "Behold how good and pleasant it is for brethren to dwell together in unity." This concord of Job's children, I do not doubt, may safely and warrantably be ascribed to God's blessings, cooperating with and giving success to Job's planting and watering of it in their religious education.

From this instance, I shall take the freedom to advise and importunately to beseech all godly parents to season their children as soon as is possible with the principles of love toward God and, in Him, toward each other, and toward all men. It is evil in itself, and worse in its consequence, to have children habituated to wrangling and contentions, and worst of all, to be encouraged and commended for brawling and fighting, especially among themselves. This counsel I give to parents, and I would entreat children to learn that lesson well that is set before them in Ephesians 4:31: "Let all bitterness and wrath and anger and clamor and evil speaking be put away from you, with all malice; and be

ye kind one to another." I shall enforce my exhortation
to both by this argument: if love is not maintained and
cherished in a family, the worship of God will be hin-
dered, the members thereof be indisposed for it, and
the blessing of God upon them will be denied or sus-
pended. For "the wrath of man worketh not the righteousness of God." The apostle willed indeed that men
pray everywhere, but with this proviso, that they do so
without wrath, as well as without doubting (1 Timothy
2:1).

Job's children conversed together, and treated one
another with great kindness. This, all will grant, was
very commendable. And they feasted together; and that
also might be done very innocently, for we do not find
that any reflections were made thereupon by the Holy
Ghost. Neither does He charge them with any disorders
committed therein. Yet Job, upon that very account, was
jealous over them with a godly jealousy, for he said, "It
may be, my sons have sinned."

Hereupon I think we may say that where there is liberal and frequent feasting, sin will be kept out with
great difficulty. That was neither an unseasonable nor
an unnecessary caution which is given by the Lord
Himself in Deuteronomy 8:11–12: "Beware that thou
forget not the Lord thy God . . . when thou hast eaten
and art full." Let the godly-wise impartially observe
whether feasting seasons do not sometimes exclude
family worship where it used to be religiously performed; or whether at least family worship is not
damnified thereby as losing much of its wonted spirit
and vigor, and degenerate into a loose, customary for-
mality. If it is really found by experience that much
feasting and family worship are indeed incompatible, I
suppose it will require no long debate which of them
should give way to the other. It is undoubtedly better
that an unnecessary feast be omitted than God be

defrauded of His worship, or the family be deprived of so great and valuable a mercy.

Job said, "It may be that my sons have sinned." It is indeed an effect of rashness and censoriousness easily to entertain groundless suspicions and evil surmises; for charity thinks no evil, but believes all things and hopes all things. But yet, in such cases as this one now before us, I suppose we may safely leave this inoffensive note: that it is very excusable that parents (either in the natural or metaphoric sense), out of their tender love and compassion, may be allowed to fear those things that have an aptitude, or but a remote probability, of endangering or hurting those who lie so near to their hearts. Upon this ground Jacob was unblameable in his solicitousness for the safety of his son Benjamin in Genesis 42:38: "If mischief befall him, then shall ye bring down my gray hairs with sorrow to the grave."

The Apostle Paul told the Corinthians that he was jealous over them with a godly jealousy in 2 Corinthians 11:2. And he told the Galatians that he was afraid for them, or on their behalf, in Galatians 4:11. Upon such an occasion as this, I hope that tender, loving, religious parents will suffer this word of exhortation. Your hearts are intimately knit to your children; you employ your uttermost care to preserve and secure them from everything that may damn or injure them; and if you are of Job's mind, you will be most afraid lest they be entangled or infected by sin. This was what made him tremble, and so earnestly to stir himself up that his sons might have sinned. You love their health and welfare in all respects; but above all see that you heartily and prudently love their souls. And therefore be careful and conscientious in making use of all those antidotes and preservatives which God has prescribed, prepared, and put into your hands to keep them from sin. You pray, it may be, in Abraham's words, "O that my child may live." Pray also with faith and fervor, and offer that petition to God which our Savior Himself has indicated in John 17:15, "I pray not that Thou shouldest take them out of the world, but that Thou shouldest keep them from the evil." Set before them fair and unblotted copies in your virtuous examples, which they may transcribe and imitate. Whet and sharpen your counsels and admonitions by serious and frequent repetitions and inculcations. With these you may plentifully furnish yourselves out of God's own book of prescriptions.

Here are a few of them, so that you may have them always ready at hand:

Proverbs 1:10: "My son, if sinners entice thee, consent thou not."

Proverbs 23:19–21: "Hear thou, my son, and be wise; and guide thine heart in the way. Be not among winebibbers, among riotous eaters of flesh. For the drunkard and the glutton shall come to poverty; and drowsiness shall clothe a man with rags."

Proverbs 13:20: "He that walketh with wise men shall be wise; but a companion of fools shall be destroyed."

Psalm 119:9: "Wherewithal shall a young man cleanse his way? By taking heed thereto according to Thy Word."

Proverbs 4:14: "Enter not into the path of the wicked; and go not in the way of evil men."

If you will exercise only a competent diligence, you may gather heaps upon heaps of such holy aphorisms. I know that tender parents have often aching hearts when they do not know where their children are; and yet they must be content to have them out of their sight. They should therefore endeavor to do that by affectionate admonition which they cannot always do by personal inspection. Warn and charge your children when grown up not only to keep out of the company of the openly profane—who have their plague-sores running upon them, and convey infection and death to all that come near them—but advise them also against intimate familiarity, and frequent unnecessary converse, with such as may be civil, witty, and obliging, but are destitute of and bitter enemies to the power of godliness; whose discourses are ordinarily compounded of levity and vanity, together with railing and sarcasm, to ridicule or reproach all that is serious or sacred. There is a fascinating malignity in some people's discourses in which the poison is wrapped up in gilded pills, and the deadly hook is covered with a pleasant bait. How sadly and commonly is that saying proven which Paul gave us, "Evil communications corrupt good manners." Some, if they please, may call this a long digression; but I am sure it leads directly to the end designed by me in drawing up this discourse, which was to promote family religion in its life and power, and so to take the opportunity to excite you unto it and direct you to the fruitful ordering and management of it, which those Scriptures that I was led to consider freely offer unto me.

A fourth circumstance that deserves closer inspection is that Job sent and sanctified his sons. This imports more than that Job prayed God to sanctify them by His grace; for it plainly insinuates that Job intended that something should be done by them toward effecting or promoting their own sanctification, in order to their participation in the use and benefit of that sacrifice which was to be offered on their behalf.

This notion of sanctification frequently occurs in the Scriptures to denote a due preparation for religious worship. When God commanded Jacob to go to Bethel to erect an altar there for sacrifices, he said unto his household, "Put away the strange gods that are among you, and be clean, and change your garments" (Genesis 35:2). This is all one as if he had said, sanctify yourselves. Thus upon that solemn occasion, when God was about to proclaim the law at Mount Sinai so that the people might be prepared to draw near to Him, He gave this charge to Moses, as found in Exodus 19:10–11: "Go unto the people, and sanctify them today and tomorrow; and let them wash their clothes, and be ready against the third day." And more expressly, 1 Samuel 16:5: "Sanctify yourselves, and come with me to the sacrifice."

This preparatory sanctification is twofold: external and ceremonial, and internal, or moral and spiritual. The external sanctification consisted in divers washings and carnal ordinances (or rites and ceremonies) imposed on them, until the time of reformation, Hebrews 9:10. The internal sanctification consisted in casting sin from the heart and life, and sincerely turning unto God. James 4:8: "Draw nigh to God, and He will draw nigh unto you; cleanse your hands, ye sinners, and purify your hearts, ye double minded." Psalm 26:6: "I will wash my hands in innocency; and so will I compass Thine altars, O Lord." Isaiah 1:16–17: "Wash ye, make you clean; put away the evil of your doings from before Mine eyes; cease to do evil, learn to do well." As this is to be done by every one personally, so, in order to family worship, the like sanctification is to be looked after. Jacob said to his household, "Be clean." This is ratified by Job 11:13–14: "If thou prepare thine heart . . . and let not wickedness dwell in thy tabernacles."

Hence we conclude that, although the ceremonial ways of preparatory sanctification ceased with the typological sacrifices, yet we are still to retain and observe the spiritual part as agreeable to spiritual sacrifices, which continue under the gospel.

The phrase of Job's sanctifying his sons being thus cleared, I conceive we may naturally and regularly draw these inferences.

Here we find a sacrifice to be offered by Job in and

for his family, to which he called his sons. This proves that there were family sacrifices. And this is yet more expressly asserted in 1 Samuel 20:6: "There is a yearly sacrifice for all the family." Our translation says "a yearly sacrifice," and I suppose the Hebrew phrase may so intend it." Yet the words literally translated are "a sacrifice of days." And so Montanus renders them, "Or sacrifices for some days are then celebrated for the whole family." But whether that sacrifice was annual or occasional, or ordinary, is not material for our purpose, seeing it is without controversy. There was a family sacrifice, and therefore there was family worship; because sacrificing was an eminent way of performing religious worship.

OBJECTION. The word translated "a sacrifice" might have been rendered "a feast for the family." It imports no more than a slaying of beasts in order to furnish provisions for a feast. Genesis 43:16: "Bring these men home, and slay (or kill a killing) and make ready, for these men shall dine with me at noon." If then this were only a family feast, then it was not a family sacrifice; and so nothing can be deduced from thence to establish or countenance family worship.

ANSWER. This is but an evasion, not a confutation. For if we admit that a feast was then kept to which the family came, yet it was not a common feast for entertainment, hospitality, or kindness, but a religious feast held with respect to the worship and glory of God. Neither should this seem strange, if we consult either the Scriptures or the customs of the heathen (who probably studied in this to imitate the Jews). In the rules and orders which were given touching sacrifices, we find that in their peace offerings the fat, having been burnt upon the altar and the priest having taken his portion, the remainders of the flesh were delivered to those who brought the sacrifice, who used therewith

to hold a feast. Observing this will help us to understand that speech of the light and lewd woman found
in Proverbs 7:14, "I have peace offerings with me; this
day have I paid my vows." That is, "I hold a sumptuous
feast today, upon the remainders of the flesh of my
peace offerings, and so I can treat thee splendidly and
plentifully."

As for the passage brought out of Genesis, that will
not befriend the cause for which it was produced, another word being there used which is proper to denote
the slaying of beasts in order to furnish a plentiful but
civil or common entertainment. So that, notwithstanding this exception, the argument remains in its full
strength and unshaken. Here we find plainly and evidently there was a family sacrifice, and that is a good
proof of family worship. Before and under the Law, typical sacrifices were acknowledged by all to have been
one of the solemn rites of divine worship. But when
Christ (the true Sacrifice which was prefigured by those
typical ones) had once offered up Himself, there was no
more any place left for them. Hebrews 7:27: "Who
needeth not daily, as those high priests, to offer up sacrifice . . . for this He did once, when He offered up
Himself." Hebrews 10:14: "For by one offering He hath
perfected forever them that are sanctified."

So that under the gospel there remains only
metaphorical or spiritual sacrifices to be offered up to
God. 1 Peter 2:5: "Ye also as lively stones are built up a
spiritual house, a holy priesthood to offer up spiritual
sacrifices acceptable to God through Jesus Christ."
Hebrews 13:15: "By Him therefore let us offer the
sacrifice of praise to God continually, that is, the fruit
of our lips, giving thanks to His name." The offering of
such sacrifices is a principal part of family worship.

In order to the family sacrifice, Job directed his sons
to sanctify, that is, to duly prepare themselves. And

from hence I infer that there ought to be a due preparation for family worship by composing our hearts to seriousness so that they may be brought into and kept in a holy frame. It is a great disparagement to family worship when we rush into it without fitting preparation, seeing we have to do with the holy and blessed God therein, as well as in any other way wherein we are to make our address to Him, and we expect that He should meet with us and bless us. Solomon advises and directs us how we are to enter upon the public worship in Ecclesiastes 5:1: "Keep thy foot when thou goest to the house of God." And we do as well need a monitor, to say to us, "Look well to your hearts when you are to perform family worship."

Job sent and sanctified his sons. That does not mean that he infused grace or holiness into them; for to sanctify, in that sense, is the prosper and peculiar work of God, who is the God of all grace, and immediately the production of the Holy Spirit (see 1 Peter 5:10; 2 Thessalonians 2:13; 1 Peter 1:2). But Job may be said to sanctify them in a way of instrumentality or subservience to God by his fervent prayers to God to bestow His saving grace upon them by instructing them, and enforcing his serious counsels and admonitions frequently upon them by setting his course of life before them as a good pattern for them to imitate, and by making use of such other ordinary means as God has prescribed, and promised to bless in order thereunto. Here also I may infer that it is a great encouragement to excite and engage holy persons to use all industry and fidelity in promoting family religion with all their might, that they may, by God's blessing, contribute very much toward the sanctification of their children and servants. What the Apostle Paul said to Timothy, (1 Timothy 4:16: "Take heed to thyself and to thy doctrine, continue in them; for in so doing, thou

shalt both save thyself and them that hear thee"), I
doubt not but that, in a way of parallel or
accommodation, I may say to religious heads of families. Follow after holiness in your hearts and lives, and
labor to instill the precepts, principles, and practices
thereof into those who are under your charge.
Continue to do so with fidelity and activity, and, by the
grace of God, you may save yourselves and them also.

A fifth remarkable circumstance is that Job offered
burnt offerings according to the number of them all,
that is, of all his sons at least, and they were seven. If we
extend this to his daughters also, there were three
more. From this passage we may observe that the history relates how Job sent and sanctified his sons so that
they might come to the sacrifices which he designed to
offer on their behalf. We may presume that they came,
being sent for by their father; and that, when they were
come, Job proceeded to offer the burnt offerings. From
hence we may learn that when family worship is to be
performed, all the members of the family should be
gotten together so that they may be present. It is then
very disorderly to have family worship performed at
such seasons as several of the family cannot come to
join therein; or that they come and are under such dis-
advantageous circumstances that they bring with them
such unavoidable indispositions that it may truly be
said of them, in a sense too obvious, that they are absent while they are present.

We can also observe that Job sent and called his
sons to the sacrifice. Hence the heads and governors of
families may be admonished to take due care that all
the members of the family be called to join in the worship to be performed, and to take notice of those who
absent themselves without a very just and allowable
cause.

The sixth circumstance which is mentioned relating to family worship is that Job offered burnt offerings according to the number of them all. Upon this I shall leave but one remark, that when parents have many children, each child particularly may challenge an interest in their care, especially in things belonging to their soul-concernments, so that they be brought up in the nurture and admonition of the Lord. Each of them should be personally instructed, watched over, and prayed for. The partiality of some parents is justly reproveable who are fondly indulgent to some of their children and neglect others. This is unnatural, as well as irreligious.

The last thing pointed at is Job's constancy in this holy work: "thus did Job continually." The word signifies "all days" or "every day." From hence I infer that what Job did in this case was not only accidental or occasional upon a present emergency, and then laid down again, but that this was his stated practice, a matter of constant use and observance.

As far then as this example of Job should influence us to perform family duties, so far it will oblige us also to be constant therein, "all days" or "every day." They then who perform them only upon some emergencies, as under some short-lived convictions, surprising providences, or feverish fits of devotion, and then intermit them or lay them aside, may be concluded not to proceed upon Job's internal principles, which were steady and uniform. Rather, they are only moved, like machines, by some alien springs or engines.

I may add one reflection more upon this occasion. As often as there is a just reason impelling and obliging us to any action or performance, so often should we excite and engage ourselves to act accordingly. This carries its own evidence and efficacy in natural things. We seek and take sustenance and refreshment for our bodies every day because we daily need them. Upon this

reason may the constant, daily performance of family
duties be enforced, because there is daily need of them.
We are to pray for daily pardon of sin, as we are directed
in the Lord's Prayer: "Give us this day our daily bread."
And then, in an inseparable conjunction therewith it
follows, "and forgive us our trespasses." To pray for
daily grace to sanctify us and daily blessings upon our
families, according to this excellent pattern: "Thus did
Job continually." And thus we arrived to the end of this
stage, the improvement of Job's example as an argument for family worship.

# 7

## *The Example of Joshua*

I shall bound the fifth period in the disposal of the times under the Old Testament from the time that Israel was brought into the possession of the Land of Promise to the end thereof. Within this interval I shall produce the famous example of Joshua, which is, I think, taken notice of by all who deal with this subject. The place chiefly fixed upon as being most pertinent and pregnant is Joshua 24:15: "But as for me and my house, we will serve the Lord." Here we have Joshua's solemn profession, protestation, and engagement, which he entered and would have recorded, that he undertook as well for his house as for himself, that not only separately, but also conjunctly, both he and his house would serve the Lord. There are but two things (as far as I can apprehend) that can be required for the illustration and application of this place to render it a manifest and irrefragable proof for family worship.

1. Joshua's "house," by a usual metonymy, undoubtedly signifies his family, and is so understood by all without one gainsayer that I know of. The Chaldean paraphrase is clear for it; for there it is rendered, "I and the men of my house will serve before the Lord." The men of his house were such as dwelt with him. That is a common Scripture phrase, as in Genesis 17:27: "All the men of his house, born in his house, and bought with money." Genesis 39:11: "There were none of the men of the house there within." This explication of "the men of my house" would have been impertinent if there had

57

been none of that temper who (as the proverb is) will feel for a knot in a bullrush. Though the Chaldean speaks plainly, yet the Syriac translation is more express, and renders the words thus: "I indeed, and my domestics, will worship the Lord God." Tremelius and Junius also say the very same terms, "But I and my family will worship Jehovah." Joshua's "house" then is his household or family, nothing being more familiar in Scripture than to call the family by the name of the house. Genesis 12:17: "And the Lord plagued Pharaoh and his house with great plagues." In the celebration of the Passover, every house, that is, every household or family, was to take and eat a lamb. Exodus 12:3–4: "They shall take to them, every man a lamb, according to the house of their father, a lamb for a house; and if the household be too little for the lamb . . . ." Nothing can be more plain than that a house and a household are here the same thing.

The reason why I insist so much upon this is because when Jeremiah 10:25 is alleged in proof of family worship ("Pour out Thy wrath . . . upon the families that call not upon Thy name"), some think it sufficient to say that "families" there are of a large signification, and as extensive as nations and kingdoms. But that evasion will not serve when the example of Joshua is made use of to the same purpose; for he speaks of his house or family in the most proper, strict, and appropriate sense, that he and his house would serve the Lord. Against this, I do not know that any exception ever has been made, and I presume cannot be made. And therefore I shall take it as a thing to be admitted and not contested.

2. We move now to the matter of Joshua's protestation, or what it was unto which he thus solemnly engaged himself. And that was that both he and his house conjunctly would serve the Lord. Neither will this meet

with any opposition that I can foresee; but if anything is stood upon, it will be, I suppose, about the meaning of that expression of serving the Lord.

Some may possibly think that herein they may find matter about which to cavil, as not being strict and close enough to tie us to family worship. For they may say that to serve the Lord is a phrase of very large meaning, is consequently ambiguous, and so will not directly conclude for family worship. The meaning then of that expression, that he and his house would serve the Lord, might be no more than this: that upon a supposition that the whole body of the Israelites should turn apostate, and forsaking the true God should worship idols or false gods, yet he was fixed in his resolution that he and his family would persevere in their faith, obedience, and worship, and cleave to Jehovah alone as their God, He being the living and true God.

I answer, let all this be admitted, yet it will not in the least invalidate the argument for family worship being grounded on Joshua's example, unless it could be shown that serving the Lord either excludes or is inconsistent with worshipping Him. Whereas I think every unprejudiced person, being guided by Scripture and reason, would think it were a fair and strong way of arguing that, if we must serve the Lord, then doubtless we must worship Him, because it is an unaccountable thing. How is it possible that they should serve God who do not worship Him? But it would be a very wild kind of reasoning to argue from serving God to the exclusion of His worship. He would be hissed at as a very illogical disputant who, by admitting the genus, should argue for the excluding of the species; as because a man is a living creature, therefore he is not a rational one.

But not to expose the weakness of that exception any further, I shall endeavor to show what advantage and improvement is to be made of the comprehensiveness of the phrase here made use of, that of "serving the Lord." This takes in all family religion in its whole compass, and the various duties therein to be attended unto, as by instruction of those who are to be seasoned with the knowledge and fear of God, keeping all the members of it under a holy rule and government, the worship of God together in holy prayers and praises and such like.

To serve the Lord undoubtedly includes and intends worshipping Him. This lies so plain and visible that both the Syriac and the latter Latin translators thought themselves warranted to render the words as "Both I and my domestics, or my family, will worship the Lord."

These phrases, "to serve the Lord," and "to worship Him," are often used interchangeably, as importing the same thing. Exodus 8:1: "Let My people go, that they may serve Me." Compare that with Exodus 5:3: "Let us go three days' journey into the desert, and sacrifice to the Lord our God." Sacrificing was then one of the most solemn rites of worship. Sometimes these two are conjoined as exegetical, one for the other. Matthew 4:10: "Thou shalt worship the Lord thy God, and Him only shalt thou serve." Many are the places of Scripture which speak of serving other gods, that is, of worshipping them. Exodus 20:5: "Thou shalt not bow down thyself to them [that is, thou shalt not worship them] nor serve them." Deuteronomy 11:16: "Take heed to yourselves, that your heart be not deceived, and ye turn aside and serve other gods and worship them." I suppose by this time that enough light shines out to scatter that mist which some might endeavor to raise by the suggestion that Joshua speaks of serving the Lord with his house, but not of worshipping Him.

Some may object that, although serving the Lord may include worshipping Him, and that in conjunction with our families, yet would the proof fall short and not reach that which is intended by those who produce it in favor of family worship. For here is nothing mentioned of reading the Scriptures, praying or praising God, or any other religious exercises.

To that I answer, let it be granted that, after the example of Joshua, we are bound to serve God together with our families. And then it will be time enough to inquire how and in what ways and what duties must be attended unto, and performed in the exercise of family worship.

We shall make very ill work of it if we make void general precepts wherein the substance of the duty is commanded because all the rules and directions about it are not specified together. The wisdom of God thought it best to give forth the indication of His will in one place, and then to employ our diligence in searching the Scripture, touching more particular discoveries of it as He shall be pleased to signify them to us.

This being a matter to signify them to us, and yet not sufficiently attended unto by many, I think it will be a good piece of service, in order to the subject we are upon, to insist a little further upon it and take into consideration a case which in many things are much like this one of family worship, and that is the sanctification of the Sabbath.

The fourth commandment lays the foundation for Sabbath worship. This, I am confident, will not be denied by any, whatever other disputes have been agitated touching the Sabbath. Let us then look to the preceptive part of that command, and it stands thus: Remember the Sabbath day, to keep it holy. There is no particular mention made of any holy duties or religious exercises to be performed by them who would sanctify the Sabbath, save only that they are to rest on that day

from all servile work, which I suppose is not accounted
by any to be all that is intended in that injunction to
sanctify the Sabbath day. But if we consult the Scriptures, we shall find several instances of such things to
be done and religious exercises performed as are
agreeable and requisite to be attended unto in order to
sanctify a day set apart for holy rest. Of these, some were
ceremonial, and consequently are but of temporary
duration; others were moral and perpetual.

Among the ceremonials exercises, we find the dou-
bling of the daily burnt offerings. Numbers 28:9–10:
"And on the Sabbath day two lambs of the first year,
without spot. . . ." This is the burnt offering of every
Sabbath, beside the continual burnt offering. From this
we may piously infer that though God is to be worshiped every day, yet more abundantly on the Lord's
Day.

But without further inquiry about ceremonials, it
concerns us to observe what is recorded in Scripture
touching the moral duties and exercises of religion
that were practiced in order to sanctify the Sabbath.
The Scriptures were publicly read in their assemblies.
Acts 15:21: "For Moses hath of old times, in every city,
them that preach him, being read in the synagogues
every Sabbath day." There was preaching, the expound-
ing and applying of some portion of Scripture. A large
account of this we have in Luke 4:16–18. Our Lord Jesus
was in Nazareth, and having read a portion or text out
of the prophecy of Isaiah, He explained and applied it,
that is, He preached upon it. So Acts 13:14–16. When
Paul and his company "came to Antioch in Pisidia, they
went into the synagogue on the Sabbath day, and sat
down. And after the reading of the law and the
prophets, the rulers of the synagogue sent unto them,
saying, 'Ye men and brethren, if ye have any word of
exhortation for the people, say on.' " And then Paul

preached his sermon, the headings whereof are there rehearsed. There were also solemn prayers offered up to God. Acts 16:13: "And on the Sabbath we went out of the city by a riverside, where prayer was wont to be made." Some learned men render those words, "where there was a *preseucha*," or an oratory (much of the same use as with a synagogue) where they assembled for prayer and other holy duties on the Sabbath days. The high praises of God were also celebrated. This is evident from Psalm 92, the title whereof is, "A Psalm or Song for the Sabbath Day." And then the Psalm begins, "It is a good thing to give thanks unto the Lord, and to sing praises unto Thy name, O Most High." This may be judged sufficient to set forth what I designed, which was to recommend this note to be well-studied and pondered by the humble, serious, and wise, so that God may give forth His command in general terms in one place, and leave us to search for particularities in other places, as is undeniable in that instance of keeping holy the Sabbath day. Proceed then accordingly in the case of serving God with our families, and you may conclude that whatsoever duties God prescribes to families, they are virtually comprehended under that general expression of serving God in and with them.

These exceptions being answered, I cannot foresee any other. And therefore, until some appear, I take it for granted that family religion is sufficiently established upon the example of Joshua. And so I shall close it with some plain and practical observations.

Joshua was a great and a good man; and the examples of such have a mighty efficacy to engage, excite, and encourage us to imitate them.

Joshua was supreme governor in the commonwealth of Israel. He did not have the name of king, but he had the regal power. What was said of Moses in Deuteronomy 33:5, that "he was king in Jeshurun," may be applied also to Joshua. And from thence I infer that it ought to be the care of great persons, as well as others, to engage themselves to uphold family religion.

Joshua must be supposed to have been encompassed with a throng of businesses, the management both of martial and civil affairs lying chiefly on him. And from hence I collect that the pretense of a multitude of business is not sufficient to discharge family duties. They who are not at leisure to worship God in their families must, when their day comes, allow themselves a time to die; for "when their breath goeth forth, they return to their earth; in that very day their thoughts perish" (Psalm 146:4). They must appear before the judgment seat of Christ, and receive according to what they have done, whether it be good or bad.

Joshua makes this supposition, "What if the body of people should turn renegades?" Even in such a case, he resolved and protested that both he and his house would serve the Lord. Hence we may be allowed to put the question, "What if the generality of those among whom we live should neglect, despise, nay, and deride family worship?" Every well-principled and every well-established Christian must resolve (in the strength of Christ) to persist and persevere in his duty. He who intends to travel heavenward must be content to hold on in his journey with a small company, because "strait is the gate, and narrow is the way, which leadeth unto life, and few there be that find it."

Joshua undertakes for himself and his family that they will serve the Lord. But in this order, that he will lead the way ("me and my house"). Family governors must be the first in promoting family worship. It is not enough for them to say to children and servants, "See that you serve the Lord." But they must say, as Zechariah 8:21, "Let us go speedily, and pray before the Lord . . . and I will go also." There are too many who walk in the steps of those lawyers, against whom our Savior denounced a dreadful woe in Luke 11:46, "Woe unto you, ye lawyers, for ye laden men with heavy burdens, and grievous to be borne, and ye yourselves touch not the burdens with one of your fingers."

Joshua engaged for his house as well as for himself that they shall serve the Lord. And in this he went no farther than he was authorized and empowered by God to go. Hence we conclude that religious governors of families have authority from God to command their household to serve the Lord. This was evidenced before from the precedents of Abraham and Jacob.

And thus I leave the example of Joshua to be imitated by all those whose hearts the Lord shall incline to undertake and persist in the advancement of family religion.

I might go on and produce more examples in this period of time, and allege what is said of David in 2 Samuel 6:20: "Then David returned to bless his household." Then, and very pertinently, I might bring in the whole of Psalm 101 as a most excellent platform, according to which a religious family may be modeled. I might also recommend to holy women the noble example of Esther, who undertook to keep a religious fast with her maidens (Esther 4:16). But I shall conclude as the apostle does his recital of examples in Hebrews 11:32. And what shall I say more? For time would fail me to tell of the rest of those whose care for family religion is pointed at in several passages of their history, or may be found among the exhortations or directions they have given regarding it.

I am very sensible that our journey through the Old Testament—which was undertaken that we might view some examples of those who have been signally eminent for their care and zeal about family worship—has been much longer than I either expected or intended.

If any reader shall complain of the length of the way, I hope it may be some refreshment to him to find that his labor has not been altogether in vain. And if he is pleased to continue, I will, for his encouragement, assure him that I will endeavor to make the remaining part of this discourse much shorter, and contract it as much as I may, without prejudice to his edification.

# 8

## *The Example of Christ*

Let us proceed to the New Testament and observe what examples for family religion are therein presented before us. I shall begin with the example of our blessed Lord and Savior, Jesus Christ. That His example is to be followed in all things that may be imitated by us will not be questioned by any who think themselves bound in duty to obey His precepts, which are many, and those are very express. 1 Peter 2:21: "Christ also suffered for us, leaving us an example, that we might follow His steps." 1 John 2:6: "He that saith he abideth in Him ought Himself also to walk, even as He walketh." And as His practice ought to be our pattern in other things, so also in His care of family religion.

It is likely that some will smile at my attempt to bring Christ's example for improving and establishing family worship. They suppose that Christ neither had nor could have any family at all, and think they have Christ's own words to confirm them in that opinion. Matthew 8:20: "The Son of Man hath not where to lay His head." Since our Savior, then, was in no capacity to have any family, he who endeavors to build upon Christ's example in this matter bestows his pains to no purpose for which in reality there is no foundation, some will say.

I have the charity to hope that they who triumph in this objection were only betrayed into this conceit through precipitancy and want of mature consideration, and that all such as study truth will relinquish

their error when discovered to them. Let us but diligently and impartially weigh what is recorded in the
evangelical history, and then I do not doubt but that it
will evidently appear that Christ both had a family and
that He upheld the worship of God in it. That I may
therefore lay open what I have to offer with the greater
perspicuity, I shall answer more distinctly.

Christ's words that the Son of man had nowhere to
lay His head were spoken on a special occasion, and are
to be understood as accommodated thereto. This may
be collected from verse 19: "And a certain scribe said
unto him, 'Master, I will follow Thee whithersoever
Thou goest." He pretended to be ready to enroll himself in the number of Christ's disciples who constantly
attended upon Him, and went up and down with Him
in His preaching the gospel. By Christ's answer we may
well conjecture upon what motive the scribe was induced to be so forward as to desire to be admitted into
His service: it was an expectation of reaping some considerable advancement of his worldly interest. We may
fairly presume that he came to Christ, accounting Him
to have been the promised Messiah whom the Jews
generally fancied would be a magnificent and victori-
ous prince. And by entering himself into His service,
he promised himself some good preferment. This I
conceive to be the true state of his case. And the answer
given him by our Savior greatly strengthens this hypothesis, for Christ plainly said to him that his design
would be frustrated and his expectations disappointed
by letting him know that He was at present in His state
of humiliation, very ill provided to gratify His followers
with worldly remunerations. They saw that He had no
royal palace to entertain them, no lands or revenues to
distribute among them, nor so much as a house of His
own for His repose and residence. In vain therefore did
this scribe seek to advance or enrich himself.

There were many others who repaired to Him upon carnal inducements. He told those who solicitously sought Him and ran after Him (John 6:26), "Verily, verily, I say unto you, ye seek Me not because ye saw the miracles [for the exciting or strengthening of your faith], but because ye did eat of the loaves and were filled." To prevent therefore all such vain and worldly hopes, our Lord frequently inculcated that such as could be content to be His disciples must learn to deny themselves, and to take up His cross and follow Him. When those things are maturely weighed, I am confident that they who from Christ's answer to the scribe were forward to conclude that our Savior neither had nor could have any household or family will perceive their argument to fail them.

It is not necessary or essential that there must be always a settled place of residence, or be fixed to one house without moving or stirring from it, to constitute a family. For then they who have many seats or houses, and reside sometimes in one, sometimes in another, should be as much incapacitated to have a family as they who have none. But that which is essential to the being of a family is the mutual relationship that is between the head and members of a family, and of the members toward one another. This has been sufficiently cleared already in the foregoing part of this discourse, in speaking to the case of Job's sons, whom some deny to have been members of his family because they had houses of their own and dwelt in various houses.

OBJECTION. Yes, we admit that it is not constant residence in one house, but mutual relationships that constitute and denominate a family; yet it does not appear that they who are supposed to have been members of Christ's family stood in any family relationship toward Him, but only in the relationship of disciples or scholars toward Christ as their Master or Teacher.

ANSWER. Many things might be produced to show a great analogy and correspondence between a school and a family. The scholars in Scripture are called the "sons of the prophets," and the teacher their "father," terms by which family relations are expressed. Thus Elisha called Elijah his father in 2 Kings 2:12. And with the same compellation did Naaman's servants address themselves to him in 2 Kings 5:13: "My father, if the prophet had bid thee do some great thing . . . ." Let anyone observe what is spoken of the schools of the prophets, and he will perceive that they differed little or not at all from their families (see 1 Samuel 19:20; 2 Kings 4:28; 6:1).

All grant that those whom we account to have been members of Christ's family were His disciples. Let us then attend to that distinction which the gospel puts between Christ's disciples, of which there were two ranks or kinds. Some were disciples at large only; others were so in a more strict or appropriate manner. And this distinction was made by our Lord Himself in Luke 6:13: "And He called His disciples unto Him, out of which He chose twelve, whom He named apostles." Mark 3:14 adds that Christ ordained that these twelve should be with Him, and always attended Him wherever He went, as His proper domestics.

Between Christ and these twelve there was not only the relationship of teacher and scholars, but also the family relationship of master and servants. This is confirmed by proofs of all kinds.

Christ supposed it in His discourse with them in Matthew 10:25: "If they have called the master of the house Beelzebub, how much more shall they call them of his household?"

The relationship between Christ and His apostles was known and taken notice of by others. Matthew

17:24: "Doth your Master pay tribute?"

This was the title which they ordinarily gave Him when they spoke to Him. John 4:31: "Master, eat." Mark 9:5: "Master, it is good for us to be here."

And the same style did they use when they spoke of Him in Mark 14:14: "The Master saith, 'Where is the guest-chamber, where I shall eat the Passover with My disciples?' "

Our Lord Himself attests and confirms this relationship in John 13:13: "Ye call Me 'Master' and 'Lord,' and ye say well, for so I am."

It would be very strange if after all these testimonies anyone should doubt whether our Lord Jesus Christ had a household or family or not.

They proceed upon a false supposition who conclude that our Lord neither had nor could have a household because He did not have a house; for the contrary may be clearly proved from Scripture. If the question were put whether had Christ a house, the answer must be that we cannot certainly determine whether (according to our law terms) He had a house or was, in the strict sense, the legal proprietor of one. We cannot know whether He rented a house, such as Paul had at Rome (Acts 28:30) or whether he was accommodated with one by some of His friends or followers; for it is certain that they provided maintenance for Him. Luke 8:3: "And many others which ministered unto Him of their substance." From whence we may in all probability conclude that they who furnished Him with other necessaries also took care of a habitation for Him.

But we need not be too scrupulous in this inquiry; it is sufficient that the Scripture assures us that our Savior had a residence. John 1:38–39: "Master, where dwellest Thou? He saith unto them, 'Come and see.' " And yet more distinctly, Matthew 4:13: "And leaving Nazareth,

He came and dwelt in Capernaum," which is therefore called "His own city" in Matthew 9:1. It could not be His own city because of His being born there; on that account Bethlehem was His own city (Matthew 2:1). Nor could it be His own city because He had His education there, for that was at Nazareth (Luke 2:51). And there is Luke 4:16: "And when he came to Nazareth where He had been brought up," which was thereupon reputed His own country. Verse 23: "Whatsoever we have heard done in Capernaum, do also here in Thy country." After Christ had entered on the solemn and public exercise of His ministry and called His disciples, He, with the twelve whom He had selected to be His constant attendants or servants, ordinarily dwelt in Capernaum, and there as a citizen or inhabitant He paid the tribute money (see Matthew 17:24 and following).

By what has been alleged, I think it is proved sufficiently that our Lord Christ had His household or family. We shall now inquire what may be produced to establish family worship from our Savior's example. Several manifest footsteps thereof are recorded for our imitation.

Besides His public preaching to His audience at large, He privately taught and instructed His own domestics. Thus He spent a great part of the night that preceded His passion with them, the breviate of which heavenly discourse is registered in chapters 13–16 of the gospel of John. Neither was this the only time that He spent in their instruction, but it was ordinary and customary for Him to do so. Here it may be of singular advantage to observe what course He took to carry on their improvement.

He questioned them about those things which they had heard from Him in His public preaching, and thereby He took an account of them, of both their attention and proficiency. Matthew 13:51: "Jesus saith unto them, 'Have ye understood all these things?' They say unto Him, 'Yea, Lord.' " Here is a leading precedent for heads of families to take an account of their children and servants, after their attendance upon the preaching of the Word. This would excite them to give more diligent heed unto the things that are spoken, when they know that they shall be asked touching the things which they have heard.

Our Savior repeated, explained, and inculcated upon them in private what He had taught them in public, and answered such questions or doubts as they propounded to Him. Mark 4:34: "And when He was alone, He expounded all things to His disciples." We find frequent mention made of His disciples' coming to Him for further clarification of such things as were not well understood by them. Matthew 15:15: "Declare unto us this parable." Mark 13:3–4: "Peter, and James, and John, and Andrew, asked Him privately, 'When shall these things be?' " And the like we find in many other places.

Let this excite and encourage children and servants, when sermons are repeated, modestly and humbly to mention such things as seem obscure or uncertain to them, and to desire to have them more clearly explained or more fully proved. And let heads of families be exhorted to meditate much on the things which they have heard so that they may better understand these things themselves, and so be enabled to teach others; and that they readily and cheerfully allow such as are teachable to ask them pertinent and profitable questions. Thus our Lord instructed His family.

Our Savior prayed with His domestics, which is another instance of family worship. Luke 9:18: "And as He was alone praying, His disciples were with Him." Though it is said that Christ was alone, yet that does not denote solitary or secret prayers, but private or family prayer. For it is said that His disciples were at prayer with Him. So that noting this circumstance was to let us know that Christ was alone, that is, that the multitude which commonly flocked after Him was not present, but His domestics only, as may more fully appear from Mark 4:10: "And when He was alone, they that were about Him . . . asked Him." The Evangelist speaks of Christ's praying alone with His disciples as a thing that was customary with Him. It is mentioned again in Luke 11:1: "And . . . as He was praying in a certain place, when He ceased, one of His disciples said unto Him," that is, one of them who had joined with Him in prayer. Thus we have Christ's example for family prayer.

Christ and His twelve disciples sang psalms together. Matthew 26:30: "And when they had sung a hymn [or psalm, at is is in the margin], they went out." I will not injure the patience of the reader by desiring him to accompany me while I make excursions to inquire what kind of hymn it was that our Savior sang with His disciples, whether it was one composed and accommodated to the paschal solemnity, or whether they sang one or more of the psalms of David. Learned men think the latter to be the most probable. And such as are best exercised in Jewish learning, from their authors tell us that it was the custom in their Paschal Feast to sing several psalms, beginning at Psalm 113 and ending with Psalm 118, which the rabbis call the "Hallel," or the praising song. Neither need we be so curious as to inquire into their modulation or in what manner they sang, whether in tunes set artificially or only in a louder or more distinct way of speaking, with some variation or inflexion of the voice, which probably, was the more ancient way of saying or singing psalms. The word used by the evangelists will not incline us to determine either one way or other; for they say only, "When they had said the hymn." Some render it, "and when they had uttered praises."

Neither need we dwell on the word translated "hymn," and discuss how it may be distinguished from a psalm or a spiritual song. For the apostle uses them as equivalents in Ephesians 5:19 and Colossians 3:16: "Speaking to yourselves in psalms, and hymns, and spiritual songs." Omitting then whatsoever may be thought dark or doubtful, this much is clear and certain: our Savior praised God with His disciples. And so, from His example, another excellent part of family worship is recommended to us.

And thus we have found three instances of family worship in Christ's example: teaching His family, His praying, and His praising God with His household. There can be no doubting whether Christ did these things with His disciples. And yet if any hesitates or questions whether these were His family, I shall add one proof more. And if that will not satisfy, I must confess that I do not understand how a conclusion can be inferred from any premises whatsoever. Then we must set all reasoning aside and refuse all manner of proofs, and go no further than express words and syllables, which some so earnestly call for not only in this case but in several other momentous doctrines and Christian practices. These, I believe, do not discern what pernicious and mischievous consequences will evidently and necessarily follow upon their hypothesis, that we receive nothing as a Scripture proof but what is set down there in so many expressed words. This is a point we may have occasion to insist upon soon, but I mention it here that I may give men the greater occasion and the more time to think seriously upon it.

The argument I intend to prove is that those disciples whom Christ privately instructed, and with whom He prayed and praised God were His family. They who ate the Passover together (according to the institution and ordinances thereof) were but one family or household. But Christ and these disciples did (according to God's institution) eat the Passover together. Both these propositions are explicitly set down in Scripture. The Passover was to be eaten by every family individually. Exodus 12:3–4: "They shall take unto them every man a lamb, according to the house of their fathers. And if the household be too little for the lamb, let him and his neighbor next to his house take it . . . ." That Christ ate the Passover with His select disciples we see in Luke 22:11: "The Master saith unto thee, 'Where is the guest chamber where I shall eat the Passover with My disciples?' " Verse 14: "And when the hour was come, He sat down and the twelve apostles with Him." If these do not consitute a proof, I despair of ever being able to prove anything.

# 9

## *The Example of Cornelius*

The second example of family worship which I produce out of the New Testament shall be the practice of Cornelius, which is recorded in Acts 10:1–2: "There was a certain man of Cesarea, called Cornelius . . . a devout man, and one that feared God with all his house." This is so plain and pregnant a proof that Cornelius maintained family worship that I cannot conceive what paraphrase can be made use of to illustrate it but the multiplying of words will rather darken it. Let such as require and call for an express place of Scripture make the experiment how the words mentioned are to be understood, if family worship is excluded. For here is something mentioned touching Cornelius besides his personal devotion. It is said that he "feared God with all his house." This clause must signify something, or else it is superfluous and impertinent, which none, I hope, will charge the Holy Ghost with.

That "all his house" signifies all his household will, I presume, be granted; unless those who think otherwise can produce a patent which confers upon them both skill and authority to make for us a new language.

To fear God with all his house at least necessarily includes his worshipping God in and with his family, because the Scripture so often uses the phrases "fearing God" and "worshipping God" indiscriminately. Psalm 66:4: "All the earth shall worship Thee." Compare that with Psalm 67:7: "All the ends of the earth shall fear Him." Here every man may see that to worship God and to fear Him are equivalent terms. So it is in several other places. 2 Kings 17:37: "Ye shall not fear other gods." Compare that with Exodus 34:14: "Thou shalt worship no other God." In that place which we have now under consideration, Acts 10:2, Cornelius is thus described as one who feared God with all his house. And another person of the same character is termed "one that worshipped God" in Acts 18:7: "And he (Paul) departed thence, and entered into a certain man's house, named Justus, one that worshipped God." I do not know what more needs to be said, or can be added to prove that Cornelius worshipped God with his family.

Instead therefore of wasting words to no purpose, I shall conclude with some profitable observations:

1. As to the extraction of this Cornelius, he was not a Jew by nature, but a sinner of the Gentiles, as the apostle makes the distinction in Galatians 2:15. Yet it plainly appears that he outstripped many Jews in his conscientious performance of religious duties, which was to his commendation, but to their conviction and shame. Hence we may learn that it is the sin and shame of many who enjoy great privileges and advantages over others who (on that account) are far inferior to these who yet go before them in practical godliness. They who now magnify themselves and despise others will be cut to the heart out of envy and indignation when they shall see such admitted into heaven and themselves excluded. This our blessed Savior represented once to us upon an instance very much like this one of Cornelius, who was a Gentile, as was that other centurion of whom he testified. Christ said that He had not found so great faith, no, not in Israel; and thereupon concludes in Matthew 8:11–12: "And I say unto you that many shall come from the east, and from the west, and shall sit down with Abraham, and Isaac, and Jacob, in the King-

dom of Heaven. But the children of the Kingdom shall
be cast out into outer darkness; there shall be weeping
and gnashing of teeth." I wish there might not be
something analogous here found among us, that God
is seriously and constantly worshipped in the families
of inferior persons, and is not so in the houses of some
who have a high reputation for their great learning or
estates, and, it may be, even for their profession of
religion.

2. As to his religion, Cornelius was a proselyte who
had come over to the Jews' religion. The proselytes are
in the New Testament called by two names. They are
called "worshippers of God." Such a one was Lydia. Acts
16:14: "A certain woman, named Lydia . . . which worshipped God, heard us." To display their coming over,
they are called "worshipping Greeks" in Acts 17:4: "And
of devout Greeks, a great multitude." To notify their religion, they are called "worshipping proselytes" in Acts
13:43: "Many of the Jews, and religious proselytes."

The Jews ranked the proselytes in two orders. There
were those whom they termed "proselytes of the
covenant," or "of righteousness." These were circumcised and observed all the rites of the Mosaic Law, as
the apostle intimates in Galatians 5:3: "I testify again to
every man that is circumcised that he is a debtor to do
the whole law." These were incorporated into the
Jewish church, and differed nothing in religion from
the natural Jews.

There were those whom they named "proselytes of
the gate," or "sojourners." These turned from idols to
serve the living and true God. But they were not circumcised; neither did they observe the Mosaic rites.
They were not only distinguished from Jews, as we see
in Acts 17:17: "Therefore he disputed in the synagogue
with the Jews, and with the devout persons," but the
Jews kept them at a distance from having so much as

free and familiar conversation with them, as Peter tells
this Cornelius in Acts 10:28: "Ye know that it is an un-
lawful thing for a man that is a Jew to keep company, or
come in to one of another nation." Though he had
turned from idols and served the true God only, yet, because he was not circumcised, nor bound himself to all
Mosaic observances, he was thought to be one who was
to be avoided. Such a worshipper of God was Cornelius,
and many others. Here note that a man may be a holy
worshipper of God, though he does not come up to the
pitch of some others in ceremonials or matters of free
observance.

These proselytes were called such as feared God.
Acts 13:16: "Men of Israel, and ye that fear God, give audience." Verse 26: ". . . children of the stock of
Abraham, and whosoever among you feareth God."
Here such as feared God are manifestly distinguished
from the men of Israel or children of the stock of
Abraham. And both these characteristics of a proselyte
are given to Cornelius, that he was a devout man, a holy
worshipper, and one who feared God. I have said so
much of the character of Cornelius regarding his
religion because I hope it might help some to
understand those passages that have been mentioned
touching them who worshipped and feared God. And
therefore I shall add only this brief note, that the fear
of God is the principle and spring of all holy worship.

As for his employment, Cornelius was a centurion,
that is, he was a captain, and had soldiers under him,
and yet he feared God with all his house. Hence we may
learn that a military profession and sincerity in religion are not incompatible. The bearing of arms does
not discharge men from worshipping God in any of
those ways that are appointed by Him. Let martial men
who are commanders copy this devout captain, who
gave much alms to the people, who prayed to God

always, and feared God with all his house. This is the character which is given of him, and attested to by the Holy Ghost. And let private soldiers take notice that serious godliness is not to be exterminated out of those who are of their rank and order. Some such Cornelius had in his company, for it is registered here in verse 7 that Cornelius called two of his household servants, and a devout soldier, of them that waited on him continually. What an excellent captain was here, who seasoned his servants and also his soldiers with the knowledge and fear of God! And happy are those servants, who have such masters, and those soldiers who have such commanders.

Look upon Cornelius as to his domestic relations. He was a godly master of a family. He was, in his personal capacity, a devout man. As to his relative capacity, he was one who feared God, with all his house. These two stand together in a very close and inseparable conjunction. As it cannot rationally be expected that he should make conscience of promoting religion in its power and practice in his family who is himself destitute of the principle thereof, so it cannot be well supposed that a truly godly person should take no care to promote the worship of God in his family. Upon this a very good interpreter leaves this remark: "It is not lightly to be passed over that the Holy Ghost bestows this eulogy upon Cornelius, that he had, as it were, a domestic church. For a true worshipper of God will not endure (as far as he can help it) that religion should be banished out of his house. How can that master of a family expect to be served and obeyed by those who are under his care and government, if he permits them to despise, affront, and provoke the great and blessed God?"

There is also one thing more which deserves our attention regarding this Cornelius: This grace was vouch-

safed to him by God that he was the first among the
Gentiles to whom the gospel was preached by God's
special appointment. The Holy Ghost bestows the
whole tenth chapter of Acts in recording many strange
and surprising circumstances that led the way unto,
and were all along conspicuous, in this blessed enter-
prise, the perusal whereof I recommend to the serious
and judicious reader. The Apostle Peter, who was employed therein, gives a large and distinct narrative of
the whole translation in Acts 11:4: "Peter rehearsed the
matter from the beginning, and expounded it by order
unto them." And he touches upon it again in the first
council that was held at Jerusalem. Acts 15:7: "Ye know
how that a good while ago, God made choice among us
that the Gentiles, by my mouth, should hear the word
of the gospel and believe." Whoever shall ponder these
things will, I am confident, think it very worthy of ob-
servation that this person who was, as the first-fruits of
the conversion of the Gentiles, should be set as a pattern of piety to them who should afterwards believe to
take care of family religion. As under the Old
Testament, Abraham, who was with his seed taken into
a covenant of peculiarity, was also signaled out for his
care about family worship, as has been at large declared
in the former part of this discourse, so also in the New
Testament, Cornelius, in whom was laid the foundation
of the gospel church of the Gentile converts, is also
commended for the same reason, and on the like account.

# 10

*The Example of Family Churches*

The third and last example which I produce for family worship out of the New Testament is that of family churches, which was hinted at toward the beginning of this discourse. If the argument for family worship deduced from them does not appear so clear and cogent in the eyes of some as to force its way into the minds of such as resolve not to yield to any save irresistible evidence, yet it is not to be despised or cast aside as useless because so many learned and godly persons have, with great confidence and zeal, persuaded and encouraged those who seriously mind religion to maintain, cherish, and exercise it in their families so that their houses may be modeled and conformed to the pattern of those domestic churches (as Calvin called them) which are mentioned in St. Paul's epistles. Whatsoever may be concluded and determined concerning these house churches, yet this much will stand firm against all assailants: God was worshipped in them. For to suppose a church, that is, any holy society, greater or smaller, to meet together that they might conjunctly make their application to God, and yet no religious worship to be performed, is to fancy a sun without light.

I am very desirous to contract this argument, and therefore I shall attempt two things only. I wish to lay the places wherein these house churches are mentioned before the reader, and join the judgment of some interpreters touching them. Then I shall make a few brief observations respecting our subject.

1. The places that speak of these domestic churches are four, and all of them are in Paul's epistles. Romans 16:5: "Likewise greet the church that is in their house." 1 Corinthians 16:19: "Aquila and Priscilla salute you much in the Lord, with the church that is in their house." Colossians 4:15: "Salute the brethren . . . and Nymphas, and the church which is in his house." Philemon 2: ". . . and to the church in thy house."

What is meant by the church in such or such a house? There are but two things that I know of that were ever offered by any as being intended by that expression. First, that by "the church in such a house," we are to understand the family so religiously framed and ordered that it might well be denominated a church. And in this channel the broadest stream runs by far. Adding some examples will, I suppose, be grateful and useful to the reader.

Romans 16:5: "The church in their house." It is a very honorable encomium when the name of a church is given to a family. And it is fitting that all the families of the faithful should be so ordered that they may be as so many little churches, said Calvin in his commentary on 1 Corinthians 16:19. Grotius (as quoted by Matthew Poole) gives not only his opinion, but also his reason: "It is credible that when Paul wrote this epistle, there were not then any common assemblies of Christians at Rome." And at such a time every house is a church. Dr. Pareus determines that the house or family of every believer, however small it is, may be called a church. Esthius (a papist), cited in Poole's *Synopsis*, declares: "The name of church, as the apostles made us of it, signifies any congregation of the faithful, though it be small and private, even of one house only."

1 Corinthians 16:19: "With the church that is in their house." It is evident that Paul commends the family of Aquila and Priscilla, as if it were a certain little

church (Beza in his *Annotations*).

Colossians 4:15: "Nymphas and the church in his house." Even a small meeting of believers, as that of a family used to be, deserves the name of a church, said Piscator. When the apostle speaks of the domestic church of Nymphas, we should take notice that in describing one family we may learn what all the families of Christians ought to be, even so many little churches.

Philemon 2: "And to the church in thy house." That is, to your whole family, which is Christian. Even three make a church, as Tertullian testifies (cited by Grotius, in Poole's *Synopsis*). The house and family of a believer, however small it is, may be called a church (Pareus).

These testimonies are sufficient to show that by the church in such or such an house, interpreters of good note understand the families themselves.

There are some who think that the houses specified are termed churches because the church or congregation ordinarily met in those houses to celebrate divine worship and to administer God's holy ordinances, such as preaching of the Word, praying, and praising God together. This opinion is mentioned by Pareus and others, but pleaded for especially by the learned Mr. Joseph Mede in his dissertation touching churches, that is, appropriate places for Christian worship both in and ever since the apostles' times. In this dissertation ["Of Churches," in *The Works of the Pious and Profoundly Learned Joseph Mede, B.D.*], he recites all the places before alleged and then thus concludes, "Which I understand not to be spoken of their families, as it is commonly expounded, but of the congregation of the saints, there wont to assemble for the performance of divine duties. I am not the first (I think) who have taken the words in such a sense. Oecumenius, in two or three of those places (if I understand him) goes the same way, though he mentions the other exposition also. As to that of Aquila and Priscilla, Romans 16, they were so eminent for virtue that they made even their house to be a church. Or this is spoken (viz., the church in their house) because all their domestics were believers, so that their house was a church."

Our very learned and pious Bishop [John] Davenant (according to the sweetness of his healing temper) is content to take in both these mentioned interpretations together, that the house of Nymphas is called a church both because the congregation used to meet there for religious worship, and also because he ordered his family in a Christian manner, and daily accustomed them to the exercises of religion.

Having thus fairly and clearly laid before the reader the judgment of learned men touching those domestic churches mentioned in Paul's epistles, I shall make a few observations upon the whole matter. I observe that expositors, both ancient and modern (as far as I understand), generally favor that interpretation which says that, in the places wherein domestic churches are spoken of, religious, well-ordered families are meant. And Mr. Mede, who would have them so denominated because the congregation used to meet in them for religious worship, ingeniously acknowledges that the places are commonly expounded to have been the families themselves. He thinks that he is not the first who took them for places where the congregation assembled. And then, that Oecumenius (if he understands him) may incline to this opinion, though he mentions the other also, which determines that families are there intended. Upon the allegation of that writer only, who is but of inferior note, both in time and esteem, I collect that if any of the more ancient or eminent doctors had anything in them to have befriended Mr. Mede's opinion, that he who was so much versed in them would undoubtedly have produced their testimonies.

I observe that if "the church in such or such a house" signifies the family, then I suppose that none can reasonably refuse this as a sufficient argument by which family worship may be established. Because if a domestic church is admitted, then of necessity family worship must come in also, for a church without worship is but a cloud without water.

I observe that though it were granted as an unquestionable thing that those domestic churches were only families, yet this can be no prejudice to the dignity, nor relax the duty, of congregational churches, who are still bound to meet for religious worship in such convenient places as the gracious providence of God is pleased to afford them, because family worship and public worship accord and embrace one another very well.

I observe that there may be a meeting for religious worship of such persons as may be denominated both a family and a congregation, in the strict acceptance of the terms; because a family may be so large and consist also of so many members as may furnish sufficient materials to constitute a congregation in which the stated worship of God may be ordinarily ministered: preaching the Word, joint prayers and praises, and holy sacraments.

Having thus discharged what I undertook, I shall conclude this part of my discourse concerning family churches with two wholesome statements from excellent Bishop Davenant:

"It rests upon every head of a family so to order and exercise his household in the true religion that his house may deservedly obtain the name of a church. Thus did Abraham, to whom God gave this testimony in Genesis 18:19: 'For I know him, that he will command his children and his household after him, and they shall keep the way of the Lord.' And Joshua 24:15:

'But as for me and my house, we will serve the Lord.'
They are unworthy of the name of Christians who (as to
religion) take no care of their domestics, but suffer
their houses to be defiled with luxury and drunkenness;
so that we may more truly call them alehouses than
churches."

Thus have I traced family worship, by its apparent
footsteps, through both the Old and New Testaments. I
grant that several other examples might have been
produced, yet those which have been alleged are abundantly sufficient to answer the end to which they were
designed, which was to manifest that family worship
was always used by the people of God. I also freely acknowledge that the examples insisted upon by me
might have been far better improved had they been
managed by a more able undertaker; all that I pretend
to is that I endeavored to render them useful to clear
the subject of the present discourse, without reflections
or exasperations of any who do not agree with me in all
points. And thus would I now very gladly put a period to
these papers which have already been carried on to a
length far beyond my intention or expectation. But I
find that I cannot as yet conclude my own pains or the
reader's patience, but must employ both a while longer
so that I may give more full satisfaction (as far as I am
able) to such as will concern themselves about a subject
of this nature.

OBJECTION. There are some who (though com-
passed about with so great a cloud of witnesses) may re-
ply upon me, "You have brought us a good store of examples, but we expect arguments, and still call for
Scripture grounds and reasons by which family worship
may be established and enforced."

ANSWER. I earnestly entreat those who make this
demand to lay aside partiality and prejudice, and to allow their thoughts and affections to judiciously weigh

the things that I humbly and freely shall lay before them. In my opinion, these things are very necessary in determining and deciding things by Scripture proofs or arguments.

Scripture examples (in those things which are therein propounded for our imitation) are very good Scripture arguments because we are commanded to follow them in our practices. This is frequently inculcated. John 13:15: "For I have given you an example, that ye should do as I have done." James 5:10: "Take, my brethren, the prophets for an example of suffering affliction, and of patience." 2 Thessalonians 3:7: "For yourselves know how ye ought to follow us." Hebrews 6:12: "That ye be not slothful, but followers of them who through faith and patience inherit the promises." But I need not produce more testimonies to assure or confirm this position.

Scripture examples in those things which are common to all the children of God have the binding power and authority of precepts because those very examples are supposed to be warranted and enforced by Divine commands. This has been done already in this discourse, especially where the example of Abraham was insisted upon. I shall therefore now dismiss it, having added our blessed Savior's admonition, upon the proposal of a good example from Luke 10:37: "Go, and do thou likewise."

Though other arguments (besides examples) should be offered, we may, notwithstanding, still be uncertain whether they will be admitted or not, if they are taken out of such topics as they who are contrary-minded shall think themselves privileged to reject at their pleasure. Unless, therefore, we resolve to continue the combat method of the *andabatae* (that is, to fight blindfolded), or, in the apostle's phrase, "to beat the air," I suppose it is very expedient that it be resolved

what arguments shall be allowed and admitted for
Scripture proofs. This is a modest and a necessary demand, because some will exact such arguments as are
not congruous to the matter under debate, and then it
will be unreasonable to say we will have such or none at
all. Others, when they are pressed with evident reasons
that militate against their opinions, retreat to this as
their stronghold: "We will have none of your reason-
ings; bring us the express words of the Scripture or we
will not be satisfied." This is a very hard case indeed,
when men will not yield to certain truth, sufficiently
and clearly proved, unless they may have the liberty to
assign and approve the arguments that shall convince
them; otherwise they will not admit them or value
them, however cogent they are.

Do men think themselves privileged by the carriage
of the Apostle Thomas, and suppose that his weakness
shall patronize all their willfulness? I am persuaded
that if some men would but attentively read and rumi-
nate upon that history which is recorded in John 20:24–
25, they would blush to see their own temper there re-
flected as in a mirror. The rest of the apostles assured
Thomas that the Lord Jesus was risen from the dead,
and that they had seen Him. But this would not satisfy
him; and he declared further that he never would be
satisfied unless it were proved in his own way: "Except I
see in His hands the print of the nails, and thrust my
hand into His side, I will not believe." I do not know at
which we may most wonder, his stiffness or his weakness. Might it not have been enough if he had seen the
wide holes made through our Savior's hands by the
great nails that were driven through them? No, but he
must also put his finger into them! Could not the gap-
ing wound made by the spear in our Savior's side speak
loud enough? No, but he must thrust his hand into it.
Alas! what is man, when he becomes vain in his imagi-

nations and disordered by his passions?

On the other hand, how astonishing was the meekness and tenderness of our compassionate Redeemer! He condescended to cure His disciple's infirmity (or rather, peevishness) in His own way. The physician signs the bill which was the patient's prescription; but withal he shows him his error, and admonishes others to beware of the like folly, which could never afterward be rectified by that application. Verse 29: "Thomas, because thou hast seen, thou hast believed. Blessed are they who have not seen, and yet have believed." They who must deal with some persons not only about the subject of this discourse, but also in many other instances, will not think this digression to be impertinent.

There are many important truths which, I trust, will be granted by all who own themselves to be Christians, to have been sufficiently proved by most strong and convincing arguments by those who produced the Scriptures to attest them, in which the conclusion that was to be proved is not to be found in the Scriptures in so many express words. This will be made more intelligible to every man's understanding by two instances (among many others that might be produced).

The Sadducees denied that there would be any resurrection of the dead. This error our blessed Savior refuted and proved the truth, which was contradictory to it, by a testimony out of the Scripture. Matthew 22:31–32: "But as touching the resurrection of the dead, have ye not read that which was spoken to you of God, saying, 'I am the God of Abraham' . . . God is not the God of the dead, but of the living." It is possible that if this proof had been brought against some of the disputants of our times, they would have rejected if not despised it, and said, "What is this to our purpose? There is not one word of the resurrection of the dead here."

But I hope that all who bear the name of Christians will pay so much reverence to the Word and wisdom of God as to acknowledge that our Lord made use of such a proof as was pertinent and adequate to that truth which He intended to confirm by it. Let us then observe His procedure in framing His argument. First, He laid down that which is asserted in the Scripture, that God (long after the time of Abraham's death) declared to Moses that He was still the God of Abraham. And then, by argumentation and deduction, He inferred the conclusion, that Abraham shall undoubtedly be raised from the dead because that person must be perfectly and completely happy who has the Lord for his God. But if Abraham should be forever kept under the power of death, he could not be perfectly and eternally happy. So here is a Scripture proof that the dead shall be raised.

Paul proved from the Scriptures that Jesus was the promised Messiah, to the conviction of unbelieving Jews. Acts 17:2–3: "And Paul . . . reasoned with them out of the Scriptures, opening and alleging that Christ must needs have suffered and risen again from the dead. And that this Jesus, whom I preach unto you is Christ."

How did he prove his assertion? He reasoned, or disputed, as a logician. His proofs, or arguments were taken out of the Scriptures. He produced his conclusion, as laid down in Scripture, not in so many express words, but as deduced from thence by necessary consequence.

Though we cannot show how or in what words he framed his argument, yet we may perceive how a solid and unanswerable argument may be formed out of the Scriptures to prove that Jesus, whom Paul preached, was the promised Messiah, who was spoken of by Moses and the prophets: He who had all the appropriate characters by which the Messiah was described and notified was undoubtedly the Messiah intended by them, and might be as certainly known thereby as if He had been expressly named. But all those appropriate characters met and terminated in that Jesus whom Paul preached, and in none other. For example, He would be born of a virgin, and the place of His birth would be Bethlehem. He would come into the world before the expiration of seventy prophetic weeks, foretold by Daniel. Messiah would be cut off; they would pierce His hands and His feet; they would cast lots on His vesture; though He was put to death, yet He would not see corruption, but would be raised the third day.

Several other such remarkable circumstances exactly and punctually centered in that Jesus whom Paul preached. Such a Scripture proof was judged sufficient by our Lord Jesus Christ Himself. Luke 24:25–27: "Then said He unto them, 'O fools, and slow of heart to believe all that the prophets have spoken. Ought not Christ to have suffered these things and to enter into His glory?' And beginning in Moses and all the prophets, He expounded with them in all the Scriptures the things concerning Himself." Paul, disputing with the Jews at Rome, took the same method. Acts 28:23: "To whom he expounded and testified the Kingdom of God, persuading them concerning Jesus, both out of the Law of Moses and out of the prophets, from morning till evening."

Upon these grounds we may maintain with great assurance that a proof drawn from the Scriptures by sound and necessary consequences is a good and sufficient Scripture proof. I recommend this axiom to all who intend to be well-established Protestants, to be maintained and held fast by them. Because it is the common artifice of the papists to unsettle and entangle those who are weak by telling them that the Protestants

cannot prove any one of their doctrines by express
words of the Scripture, such as that the Pope of Rome is
not Christ's Vicar on earth, or that the bread in the
Lord's Supper is not transubstantiated into the true,
real body of Christ; and so it is with all the rest. If the
arguments we make use of are truly drawn out of the
Scripture, and are never so plain and full, yet they
clamor, "Bring us the express words of the Scripture!" It
is unaccountable with what confidence they can challenge the Protestants to bring express Scripture for
their doctrines or else their arguments are of no validity, when in the meantime they confess that purgatory,
withholding the cup of the Lord's Supper from the laity
(as they call them), and several others, are not mentioned at all in the Scripture, nor can be proved by arguments drawn from thence, but only by tradition or
the church's authority.

I am the more insistent upon this because I think it
very needful to advise some who profess the religion of
the Protestants to consider whose work they are carry-
ing on (though I believe without any such design)
when they tell us they will admit of no proofs by argument or consequences drawn out of the Scriptures, but
press for the words and syllables of the conclusion to
be shown them in the Scripture. This is that drug
which the papists rejoice to see planted and watered
among the Protestants. This is a device in which they
greatly triumph and glory. And among them one
Francis Veron, a Frenchman, seems transported beyond all bounds of modesty. He has written a book
upon this subject. And to raise men's expectation of his
performances therein, he puts on his trappings and ti-
tles: "Reader in the King's Schools, Doctor of Divinity,
Preacher to the King, Deputed by the French Clergy to
be the Writer in Controversies." These are enough to
speak a person great and excellent. And to magnify this

rare invention, he calls it "the muzzle of the ministers," and assures us that if this engine is well-managed and handsomely applied, according to this new art (as he calls it) the very foundation of Protestantism may be easily demolished and erased.

If any shall blame me for straying thus from my subject, I did not know how to come to the end of it without fetching this compass about. Neither could I understand to what purpose it would be to multiply more Scripture grounds and reasons for the establishing and enforcing of family worship until men will receive Scripture arguments as good Scripture proofs.

# 11

*The Remaining Arguments for Family Worship*

And now, though a sufficient number of Scripture arguments for family worship have been scattered up and down throughout this whole discourse, yet, having endeavored to bring to an issue the question of what arguments ought to be accepted and admitted for Scripture proofs, I shall (to make full measure, and running over) offer some more of them. But, bearing a due respect to the reader's disposition, avocations, or occasions, I shall propound them more succinctly; forbearing copious explanations and enlargements. And I hope this brevity will not be interpreted as a diminution of the validity or weight of them.

1. I shall argue from the nature and constitution of families, in which they who thoroughly inquire into them may easily discover plain indications that the most wise and holy God cast them into such a mold that they might perceive that He intended and expected to be worshipped in them. If any think it strange that I refer families to a divine institution, and would have them cast only under His common providence, they may take notice that, though they were acknowledged to have some foundation in nature, yet that is not sufficient to make them incapable of a Divine institution. Upon due consideration, it will be found that a marriage relation is much of the same nature. Marriage, as it comes in under the law or regulation of common providence, is diffused and reaches all mankind; and yet it is an ordinance of God, sanctified and blessed in

His church and people, and is to be esteemed sacred among them (the papists indeed raise it a step too high when they advance it to the dignity and mystery of a sacrament). The case is much the same with families. They are planted all over the world. But the institution of a religious family is, by God's appointment, made over to those only who are called by His name; and so they become holy societies among whom God vouchsafes His gracious presence, and commands His blessing to abide forevermore.

Religious families being of divine institution, let us observe how that by their very constitution we may perceive an engagement to be laid upon them to worship God together; and they are excellently molded and qualified in order thereunto.

They are joined together in one society by the bond of mutual relation, which obliges them to seek and promote the good and welfare of each other according to their respective and mutual relations. Nature directs and engages them thereunto in all things of outward concern, and sets a very black mark upon them who are without natural affection (Romans 1:31). The case of that people must be exceedingly sad and deplorable among whom not only religion, but humanity also, is violated. When things had grown to such a height of impiety among the Jews, the prophet broke forth into that bitter lamentation found in Lamentations 4:3: "Even the sea monsters draw out their breasts to their young ones; the daughter of My people is become cruel, like the ostriches in the wilderness." What the reason was, why he compared them to ostriches, is rendered in Job 39:14–16: "The ostrich leaveth her eggs in the earth . . . and forgetteth that the foot may crush them, or the wild beast may break them; she is hardened against her young ones as if they were not hers." I could heartily wish that there were no cause for the like complaint among us. But, alas, there are too many who cast off the care of their families and give themselves to idleness, spending all that they earn, and more, in gaming and debauchery while their wives and children are reduced to want and extreme necessities. And unless some remedy is found and applied to put a stop to these disorders, it will be no wonder if our poverty comes as one who travels and our want as an armed man (Proverbs 24:34). The design of this discourse being to promote religion in families, I think it is very pardonable to have mentioned this plague of families which is destructive to them in all things that concern their welfare and prosperity.

And now I shall carry the argument further. If nature teaches and binds all the members of a family respectively to seek the soundness and prosperity of the whole, as to bodily welfare, grace should direct and impel them as potently to look after the safety and salvation of their souls, which are to be secured by the fear and service of God, and the enjoyment of His favor and blessing. It is an evident truth that one soul is worth more than the whole world.

Families are so disposed that they have many opportunities and great advantages to assist and encourage one another in the exercises of religion, in regard to their frequent coming together, more than any other societies are capable of. They meet usually at the times of refreshment, by food, or rest. So that, as our Savior said in another case, they may whensoever they will, do one another good (Mark 14:7). This argument is pointed at by God Himself. When He enjoins heads of families diligently to instruct their children, He insinuates the opportunities and advantages which they have so to do. Deuteronomy 6:7: "And thou shalt teach them diligently unto thy children, and thou shalt talk of them when thou sittest in thine house, and when thou walkest by the way, and when thou liest down, and when thou risest." None then can pretend that they are willing, but they lack opportunity; for that is nigh them even in their hands. And if willingness is in their hearts, nothing hinders them from making use of it.

God has made abundant provision for the securing and promoting of family worship in the duties and particular exercises thereof, both by precepts and direction. Deuteronomy 6:7: "Thou shalt diligently teach thy children." Ephesians 6:4: "And ye, fathers, provoke not your children to wrath, but bring them up in the nurture and admonition of the Lord." Proverbs 22:6: "Train up a child [in the margin, catechize a child] in the way which he shall go, and when he is old, he will not depart from it."

Many like injunctions have been occasionally mentioned in this discourse. And instead of repeating or reinforcing them, I desire to propound one more thing which possibly does not so ordinarily fall under our notice, and entreat the godly, wise, and judicious to exercise their thoughts upon it.

I humbly conceive that it may be esteemed as one signal instance of God's care for the maintaining and promoting of family religion that He commended the sanctification of the Sabbath to families in the first place, and then to magistrates who are also to look after the strangers within their gates. The fourth commandment is, "Remember the Sabbath day to keep it holy." And in order to keep it holy, we are to refrain from everything that may violate it. "Thou shalt do no work, thou nor thy son, nor thy daughter, nor thy manservant, nor thy maid-servant." The head of the family is, in a great measure, responsible for those under his charge, and ought not to suffer them to profane it, as far as he can hinder them. It is true, he cannot put grace into them to enable them to sanctify it in the ex-

ercise of internal and spiritual principles. Yet he may
see that they spend the day in the public and private exercises of God's worship, or at least he may restrain
them from profaning the Sabbath. Here let experience
be heard to testify, whether family worship and the
sanctification of the Sabbath do not ordinarily thrive or
decline together. If they find it so in the event, they
who would preserve family worship in its vigor should
be more vigilant over their families, to prevent Sabbath
profanations which will hardly be kept out if remissness and loose indifference are once let in, because
such a frame of spirit will prey upon the very vitals of religion. If family order were more inviolably observed,
and family government and power more vigorously ex-
erted, the civil magistrate would not find so many profane Sabbath-breakers. But if family governors will continue remiss and negligent herein, it is high time for
pious magistrates to put forth the zeal of Nehemiah, to
contend with the nobles (as well as the inferior people)
and to say unto them, "What evil thing is this that ye do
in profaning the Sabbath day? Did not your fathers
thus, and did not God bring this evil upon us and upon
this city? Yet ye bring more wrath upon Israel by profaning the Sabbath" (Nehemiah 13:17–18).

Every family is, by its constitution, so united, and every member, by mutual relations, so knit together that
it becomes one body; and all are joint-sharers in the
welfare or misery of the whole society. It is with a family
in this respect as it is with the natural body, as seen in 1
Corinthians 12:26: "Whether one member suffer, all the
members suffer with it; or one member be honored, all
the members rejoice." Thus it is in political bodies.
Achan, by his trespass, brought down wrath on all
Israel (Joshua 7:24–26). "Surely at the commandment of
the Lord, this came upon Judah, to remove them out of
his sight, for the sins of Manasseh . . . which the Lord

would not pardon" (2 Kings 24:3–4: ). It is true in ecclesiastical societies, according to 1 Corinthians 5:6: "Know ye not that a little leaven leaveneth the whole lump." Verse 13: "Therefore put away from among yourselves that wicked person."

This also may be experimented in domestical societies, and the rather because their conjunction and union is narrower and stricter, and therefore more directly and immediately and sensibly touched and affected. When evil is found in a family, all the members are sharers in it, whether it is the evil of sin or suffering. There may be found family sins too frequently in which the whole body may be guilty. In Jeremiah 7:18, the children, fathers, and women are all involved in the same guilt. Proverbs 29:12: "all his servants are wicked." Or if some only are actually and personally criminal, yet the rest may be partakers in those sins either by consent, or if they do not in their place and station sue for pardoning mercy, as Job did, who offered burnt offerings for the expiation of family sins.

As for family reformation, we have Jacob's example in Genesis 35:2: "And Jacob said unto his household, 'Put away the strange gods that are among you, and be clean.' " To this we may add Zophar's wholesome advice from Job 11:14: "Let not wickedness dwell in thy tabernacles."

As the evil of sin may spread to the whole family, so may the evil of suffering involve all. Genesis 12:17: "And the Lord plagued Pharaoh and his house with great plagues." Proverbs 3:33: "The curse of the Lord is in the house of the wicked." On the other hand, if the family serves God religiously, all the members may partake of God's blessings. 2 Samuel 6:11: "The ark of the Lord continued in the house of Obed Edom . . . and the Lord blessed Obed Edom, and all his household." Proverbs 3:33: "The Lord blesseth the habitation of the just."

This may suffice for that Scripture argument for
family worship, which is drawn from its constitution
and the joint participation of all the members, in the
good or evil of the whole.

2. The second Scripture argument for family worship may be drawn from the duty, the holy principle,
and the benign disposition of such as are truly godly,
and may be thus formed: Every godly man is bound to
do all the good he can, according to his calling, capacity, and relation; for every godly man should be ready
for every good work (2 Timothy 2:21). It is most evident
and undeniable that much good may be done by a
godly man in the faithful discharge of his relative duties. For the Scripture very earnestly presses to the discharge of them, and gives many directions about them,
in regard that the power of godliness is therein exercised and evidenced. You read much of the relative duties of husbands and wives, parents and children, masters and servants, which are to be conscientiously observed, as well as any other divine commands. It is then
very odd and unbecoming to hear any persons who profess godliness speak jestingly or sportingly about any of
the instances of conjugal duties. However unwise and
unwary men may make a mockery of them, yet it is certain that the power of religion displays itself in much
brightness and excellency when its professors serve
God sincerely and diligently in their proper stations.
And it is a great blemish to religion when they are
faulty and justly reprovable on such accounts.

Some examples will make this more intelligible.
When a religious man is clothed with the power and
authority of a magistrate, it is not enough for such a
one to serve God as a good man by living soberly, righteously, and godly. He must also serve God as a good
magistrate. Those are very excellent qualifications
which are to be entrusted with the magistracy, that they

be able men, such as fear God, men of truth, hating covetousness (Exodus 18:21). And when they come to execute their office, they ought to act with resolution. 2 Samuel 23:3: "He that ruleth over men must be just, ruling in the fear of God."

He who is entrusted with the office of a minister of the gospel must not think it sufficient that he is exemplary in such graces as would be very resplendent in a private Christian. But he must also take heed to his doctrine as well as to himself. He must preach the Word, be instant in season and out of season; rebuke, reprove, exhort with all long-suffering and doctrine, that he may be a good minister of Jesus Christ. It is frequently (and truly) said that every master of a family should be a prophet, a priest, and a king in his own house.

As a prophet, he is not only to teach himself, as every good man ought to do after the psalmist's example (Psalm 16:7: "My reins also instruct me in the night-seasons"), but also to teach his family (Deuteronomy 6:7: "Thou shalt diligently teach thy children").

As a priest, he is not only to present his body a living sacrifice (Romans 12:1), holy, acceptable to God, and to offer up spiritual sacrifices acceptable to God by Jesus Christ (1 Peter 2:5), but also to be, as it were, a priest for his family in things pertaining unto God, as Job offered burnt offerings for the expiation of family sins and Abraham prayed for Ishmael, and our blessed Savior prayed both for His select disciples (who were His family) and with them as their mouth to God.

As a king, he is not only to rule his own spirit, and to subdue inordinate affections and passions (on which account, "He that ruleth his spirit is better than he that taketh a city" Proverbs 16:32), but also to rule well his own house, having his children in subjection (1 Timothy 3:4). He is to command his children and his household to keep the way of the Lord (Genesis 18:19). He who conscientiously attends to and endeavors faithfully to discharge his duty in these three capacities will not stand in need of any more arguments to press him to the performance of family worship.

3. The third argument for family worship may be drawn from those many injunctions that charge the people of God not to socialize with the carnal or profane ones of the world. For God will have a separation be made between the precious and the vile, and cautions those who have His name upon them (Jeremiah 15:19; Romans 12:2) that they be not conformed to this world in evil manners, either doing that which is sinful because others do so—though they think it strange that they run not with them into the same excess of riot, and for that reason will speak evil of them (1 Peter 4:4)—or in not doing that which God has made their duty simply because others may hate or despise them for it. In such cases they must fortify themselves in Joshua's resolution: "But as for me and my house, we will serve the Lord" (Joshua 24:15). Many and strict are the Scripture commands that enforce this. Ephesians 4:17: "I say therefore and testify in the Lord that ye henceforth walk not as other Gentiles walk in the vanity of their mind." There is an abundance of other passages.

Apply this argument, and it will strongly conclude for family worship. For if those who call themselves Christians do not worship God in their families, what difference is there (in this respect) between their houses and those of the most barbarous nations or the dens of robbers? How will they be able to answer our Savior's question, "What do ye more than others?" (Matthew 5:47).

But what if some should say, "Though we have no family worship, yet we closely follow our employments, and do not ordinarily allow excess and intemperance to enter into them, even if sometimes the holy and dreadful nature of God may chance to be blasphemed, and foolish and filthy talking are connived at and other small irregularities." Are these such innocent guests that they may be safely entertained in their houses? Has not the wrath of God for these things come upon the children of disobedience, not only in personal judgments but also in family curses?

But suppose that all things in their houses were very regular; yet if they do not worship God in them, the question will return. What is there that may distinguish their families from those of sober heathens? If the destroying angel were to pass through a town or street wherein Christians and pagans dwell together, it may well be feared that he would not distinguish the houses of those who are called Christians, if God is not worshiped in them, from the habitations of others, observing no sign of God's special presence in them or any family worship daily offered up to Him. There will, at the last day, be made a manifest separation between the sheep and the goats. And it is doubtless for the interest and comfort of those who hope then to be placed at the right hand to be careful to observe all those things whereby God would have them now to keep themselves apart from them who are to be set on the left hand.

4. A fourth argument for family worship may be drawn from the principles and sentiments of nature, especially when they are approved and invigorated by Scripture. Nature teaches us to seek the good of others as well as our own. This was a maxim greatly valued among the heathen: "No man is born for himself; our country, our relatives, our friends do all claim a share in us." The Scripture enlarges it further in Galatians 6:10: "As we have therefore opportunity, let us do good unto all men." Drive home this argument. If family

worship were religiously maintained, unspeakable is the good that might be done. The apostle, though it were in a matter not very pleasant, thought he needed to say no more to persuade to compliance than this, "How knowest thou, O man, whether thou shalt save thy wife?" (1 Corinthians 7:16). This argument carries as much evidence and efficacy to bind and encourage us to family worship. In the sincere, hearty, and vigorous exercise thereof, who knows but the children and servants may find the salvation of their souls (through the grace and blessing of God) to be sensibly promoted? For thereby they will be principled in the fundamentals of religion, and also fortified against pernicious errors. They will be seasoned with the favor of religion, and be habituated and accustomed to the duties and exercises thereof. They will be disposed, and exceedingly better capacitated, to profit by the ordinances of God when publicly administered. They will, by the grace of God, be given an antidote against the poisonous insinuations and evil examples of the loose and profane. And by this means religion will be preserved and transmitted to the succeeding generation.

5. The last argument I shall mention to recommend family worship shall be the great service which it may do to the church of God and to the commonwealth, in which, by the providence of God, we are to have our repose during our stay in this world.

With respect to the church of God, he who does not heartily love the church does not sincerely love Christ Himself. For the church is His spouse, the Lamb's wife. It is His body, the fullness of Him "that filleth all in all." Many are the gracious promises that are made to them who seek and advance its prosperity. And all the genuine members thereof will naturally render it all the assistance which they can regularly contribute to it.

Now, it is evident that none can more directly and

really befriend the church of Christ than they do who
are most diligent and faithful in promoting family worship. For they replenish the nurseries with excellent
plants which may in due time be removed into the or-
chard of the church. They polish and make ready those
living stones, which are laid in the spiritual building of
the temple of God.

Neither will the commonwealth be left indebted to
them who, in their families, breed its most useful
members. For they who are religiously trained up under
family government will there learn to be modest, humble, obedient, diligent, and frugal. That kingdom
which is well stored with such citizens is in the most
hopeful way to flourish of any in the world. Were family
government more carefully maintained and exercised,
many pernicious disorders would be prevented. Let experience declare whether the greatest numbers by far of
the debauched and rapacious do not issue out of profane and irreligious families. But if any who have had
their education in these seminaries of virtue should
prove to be degenerate plants (as there may be some
rotten kernels in the fairest pomegranates), their vices
must be condemned as inexcusable and monstrous.
And if their crimes bring them under the correction of
justice, all must grant that the magistrate's hand
should fall most heavily upon them. And yet, out of
compassion to them, I heartily beseech the Lord to
awaken their consciences and to reinforce their former
instructions upon their hearts, so that they may be
brought to sincere and saving repentance, and that to
be made so conspicuous and signal as somewhat to
abate the scandal which they, by their exorbitances,
have brought upon religion. By this others, being
warned by their example, may learn and fear, and do no
more wickedly.

These, among others, are, I humbly conceive, sufficient Scripture grounds and reasons upon which family worship may be established and enforced.

And thus I have (through the help of Christ), according to my weakness, endeavored to return an answer to the question propounded to me. If any expect that I should have continued this discourse, and to have added exhortations, motives, and directions, and answered several questions or resolved the doubts and cases that relate to family worship, I must desire them to remember (as I have before intimated) that I was directed only to answer one question, and not to write a treatise. And yet I have taken as many advantages as I could fairly lay hold upon to intermingle several of those things throughout the context of this discourse. And if this mean work shall yet be esteemed imperfect, I hope the Lord will stir up some others of greater abilities to give them further satisfaction. In the meantime, if what I have done may be useful toward the clearing or establishing of the thing itself, I shall greatly rejoice. I have only been employed to lay the foundation; may others build upon it and prosper. Such as it is, I commit it to the good providence of God, and pray that His blessing may accompany it.

# 12

*Some Arguments for Performing Family Worship
Both Morning and Evening*

1. The first argument is from the light of nature, which, as it dictates to all men that there is a God, so also that this God ought to be worshipped. If He is to be worshipped, then there must be allowed times and seasons for this worship. And these times and seasons are especially when we enter upon any work which needs God's help to assist us in doing it, or His blessing to make it prosperous. Therefore morning prayer is due to God by the light of nature, when men enter upon the work of the day. Evening prayer is due to God so that men may have rest and protection in the night, and be better enabled in the work and duty of the following day. And to both of these is to be added thanksgiving, which is part of divine worship due to God also in the light of nature, and for which we have occasion and reason every morning and every evening.

2. The second argument is from the first division God made of time, which is into morning and evening. Therefore God is then especially to be acknowledged in this wise distribution of time for the use and benefit of man. So that "day unto day uttereth speech, and night unto night teacheth knowledge." And we are especially to take notice of these times wherein God is teaching and speaking to us.

3. The third argument is from the Scriptures of both the Old and New Testament. In the Old Testament we

read of the morning and evening sacrifice, which has a moral as well as a typical significance: God is to be worshipped morning and evening. The psalmist speaks of showing forth God's lovingkindness in the morning and His faithfulness every might (Psalm 92:2). And David said, "At morning, noon, and evening will I pray" (Psalm 55:17), which includes this morning and evening prayer.

In the New Testament we are commanded to pray continually, not as the Euchites or Muslims, but a constant course of prayer is intended; and a constant course of doing a thing is expressed by doing it day and night. It is said of Anna that she continued in prayer and fasting night and day (Luke 2:37). And Paul was "night and day praying exceedingly" (1 Thessalonians 3:10). The widow indeed continued in supplication night and day. And some think, when the apostle said, "Pray continually," he was alluding to the morning and evening sacrifice which is called the continual burnt-offering. The Jews had their hours of prayer, which were at least twice a day.

4. The fourth argument is from the general practice of the godly in all ages. Great regard ought to be had to it, lest by doing otherwise we give offense against the generation of the righteous and do that which is not of good report, which the apostle cautions us against in Philippians 4:8.

5. The fifth argument is from the apostle's exhortation in Philippians 4:6: "In everything let your supplications be made known to God with thanksgiving," which cannot imply less than morning and evening prayer and thanksgiving.

6. The sixth argument for family worship is because every man is obliged to promote the worship of God to his power within that sphere wherein God has set him. Masters of families are to do it in their sphere. Joshua

said, "Me and my house will serve the Lord," (Joshua 24:15), which implies a constant course of service.

7. The seventh argument is that God is to be acknowledged in all our ways so that He may direct our steps (Proverbs 3:6). This cannot imply less than morning and evening worship.

8. The eighth argument is that we are to come to the throne of grace for mercy in every time of need. And we have need of mercy especially every morning and every evening (Hebrews 4:16). This is mercy well-timed, as the Greek word imports in that place.

But I do not deny that in many circumstances of religion we are left to Christian prudence. Nor do I deny that under the gospel we are not put unto circumstances of time, times, and seasons as under the law regarding circumcision, the Passover, fasting, festivals, and so on. But what Christian prudence does direct may most conduct the honor of God; and the interest of religion is not an indifferent thing, and therefore a law. And so morning and evening worship is here made a duty.